indian

...made simple

This edition published in 2011
LOVE FOOD is an imprint of Parragon Books Ltd

Parragon
Chartist House
15-17 Trim Street
Bath BA1 1HA, UK
www.parragon.com

ISBN: 978-1-4454-3056-0

Printed in China

Created by Ivy Contract
Photography by Charlie Paul

Notes for the Reader

This book uses imperial, metric, or US cup measurements. Follow the same units of measurement through-out; do not mix imperial and metric. All spoon measurements are level: teaspoons are assumed to be 5 ml, and tablespoons are assumed to be 15 ml. Unless otherwise stated, milk is assumed to be full fat, eggs and individual vegetables are medium, and pepper is freshly ground black pepper.

The times given are an approximate guide only. Preparation times differ according to the techniques used by different people and the cooking times may also vary from those given. Optional ingredients, variations or serving suggestions have not been included in the calculations.

Recipes using raw or very lightly cooked eggs should be avoided by infants, the elderly, pregnant women, convalescents, and anyone suffering from an illness. Pregnant and breastfeeding women are advised to avoid eating peanuts and peanut products. Sufferers from nut allergies should be aware that some of the ready-made ingredients used in the recipes in this book may contain nuts. Always check the packaging before use. Vegetarians should be aware that some of the ready-made ingredients used in the recipes in this book may contain animal products. Always check the packaging before use.

indian

introduction	4
chicken	6
meat	32
fish & seafood	72
vegetables & pulses	102
snacks & accompaniments	144
desserts	186
index	208

introduction

Nowadays supermarkets stock ingredients from across the world and city streets are lined with restaurants representing every imaginable country. In the West, Indian cooking is among the most popular of eastern cuisines, especially now that keen home cooks have discovered how easy it is to prepare authentic, tasty, and nutritious Indian dishes. Perhaps the secrets of its popularity are its subtlety and extraordinary variety.

Given that the subcontinent is so huge with an equally extensive history, it is hardly surprising that both its peoples and their diets are so diverse. Religious practices have had a profound influence—Hindus don't eat beef, Muslims don't eat pork, and Buddhists, among others, are vegetarian. Explorers, conquerors, and colonizers have had an effect, too, clearly seen in the rich-tasting dishes created for Moghul emperors or the use of vinegar in the curries of former Portuguese territories, for example. Foreign ingredients are most often seen in the dishes of western India. Climate and topography play their part and each region of the country has a unique style of cooking based on local ingredients. In the north, dairy products, such

as yogurt and ghee (clarified butter), are featured, as well as nuts, while southern cooking is characterized by its use of coconuts, their oil, and a variety of chiles. Eastern regions are famous for their fish dishes and mustard oil. Delhi is well known for tandoori cooking, Kashmir for its meat, especially lamb, Madras for its wealth of vegetarian dishes, and Bengal for fine fish and tooth-achingly sweet desserts.

However, the cuisines of all regions are united in the use of careful blends of spices, which are usually bought whole and ground as needed. These mixtures are subtle and aromatic but not invariably hot, although both fresh and dried chiles do feature in many dishes. With such a wide variety of choice, why not let Indian cuisine add a touch of spice to your culinary repertoire?

chicken

chicken dopiaza

ingredients

serves 4

1 lb 9 oz/700 g skinless, boneless
    chicken breasts or thighs
juice of ½ lemon
1 tsp salt, or to taste
5 tbsp sunflower oil or olive oil
2 large onions, coarsely chopped
5 large garlic cloves, chopped
1-inch/2.5-cm piece fresh ginger,
    coarsely chopped
2 tbsp plain yogurt
1-inch/2.5-cm piece cinnamon
    stick, halved
4 green cardamom pods, bruised
4 cloves
½ tsp black peppercorns
½ tsp ground turmeric
½–1 tsp chili powder
1 tsp ground coriander
4 tbsp canned crushed tomatoes
⅔ cup warm water
½ tsp sugar
8 shallots, halved
1 tsp garam masala
2 tbsp chopped fresh cilantro
    leaves
1 tomato, chopped
Indian bread, to serve

method

1 Cut the chicken into 1-inch/2.5-cm cubes. Add the lemon juice and half the salt and rub well into the chicken. Cover and let marinate for 20 minutes.

2 Heat 1 tablespoon of the oil in a small saucepan over medium heat, add the onions, garlic, and ginger, and cook, stirring frequently, for 4–5 minutes. Let cool slightly. Add the yogurt, and blend to a paste.

3 Heat 3 tablespoons of the remaining oil in a medium heavy-bottom saucepan over low heat, add the cinnamon stick, cardamom pods, cloves, and peppercorns, and cook, stirring, for 25–30 seconds. Add the yogurt mixture, and cook for 5 minutes.

4 Add the turmeric, chili powder, and coriander and cook, stirring, for 2 minutes. Add the tomatoes and cook, stirring, for 3 minutes. Increase the heat slightly, then add the marinated chicken and cook, stirring, until it changes color. Add the warm water, the remaining salt, and the sugar. Bring to a boil, then reduce the heat to low, cover and cook for 20 minutes.

5 Heat the remaining oil in a small pan, add the shallots, and stir-fry. Add the garam masala, stir the shallot mixture into the curry and simmer. Add the fresh cilantro and chopped tomato and remove from the heat. Serve immediately with Indian bread.

chicken korma

ingredients

serves 4

1 chicken, weighing 3 lb/1.3 kg
1 cup butter
3 onions, thinly sliced
1 garlic clove, crushed
1-inch/2.5-cm piece fresh
    ginger, grated
1 tsp mild chili powder
1 tsp ground turmeric
1 tsp ground coriander
½ tsp ground cardamom
½ tsp ground cinnamon
½ tsp salt
1 tbsp chickpea flour
½ cup milk
2 cups heavy cream
fresh cilantro leaves,
    to garnish
freshly cooked rice, to serve

method

1 Put the chicken into a large pan, cover with water, and bring to a boil. Reduce the heat, cover, and simmer for 30 minutes. Remove from the heat, lift out the chicken, and set aside to cool. Reserve ½ cup of the cooking liquid. Remove and discard the skin and bones. Cut the flesh into bite-size pieces.

2 Heat the butter in a large pan over medium heat. Add the onions and garlic and cook, stirring, for 3 minutes, or until softened. Add the ginger, chili powder, turmeric, ground coriander, cardamom, cinnamon, and salt and cook for 5 minutes. Add the chicken and the reserved cooking liquid. Cook for 2 minutes.

3 Blend the chickpea flour with a little of the milk and add to the pan, then stir in the remaining milk. Bring to a boil, stirring, then reduce the heat, cover, and simmer for 25 minutes. Stir in the cream, cover, and simmer for 15 minutes.

4 Garnish with cilantro leaves and serve with freshly cooked rice.

kashmiri chicken

ingredients

serves 4–6

seeds from 8 green cardamom
  pods
½ tsp coriander seeds
½ tsp cumin seeds
1 cinnamon stick
8 black peppercorns
6 cloves
1 tbsp hot water
½ tsp saffron threads
3 tbsp ghee or vegetable oil
1 large onion, finely chopped
2 tbsp garlic and ginger paste
generous 1 cup plain yogurt
8 skinless, boneless chicken
  thighs, sliced
3 tbsp ground almonds
generous ⅓ cup blanched
  pistachios, finely chopped
2 tbsp chopped fresh cilantro
2 tbsp chopped fresh mint
salt
toasted slivered almonds,
  to garnish
Indian bread, to serve

method

1 Dry-roast the cardamom seeds in a skillet over medium–low heat, stirring continuously, until you can smell the aroma. Repeat with the coriander and cumin seeds, cinnamon stick, peppercorns, and cloves. Put all the spices, except the cinnamon stick, in a spice grinder, or use a pestle and grind to a powder.

2 Put the hot water and saffron threads in a small bowl and set aside. Melt the ghee in a flameproof casserole over medium–high heat. Add the onion and sauté, stirring occasionally, for 5–8 minutes. Add the garlic and ginger paste and continue stirring for 2 minutes.

3 Stir in the ground spices and the cinnamon stick. Remove from the heat and mix in the yogurt, a small amount at a time, stirring vigorously, then return to the heat and continue stirring for 2–3 minutes, until the ghee separates. Add the chicken pieces.

4 Bring to a boil, stirring continuously, then reduce the heat to low, cover, and simmer for 20 minutes. Stir in the ground almonds, pistachios, saffron with its soaking liquid, half the cilantro, all the mint, and salt to taste. Re-cover the casserole and continue simmering for about 5 minutes, until the chicken is tender and the sauce is thickened. Sprinkle with cilantro, and slivered almonds, and serve with Indian bread.

balti chicken

ingredients

serves 6

3 tbsp ghee or vegetable oil
2 large onions, sliced
3 tomatoes, sliced
½ tsp nigella seeds
4 black peppercorns
2 green cardamom pods
1 cinnamon stick
1 tsp chili powder
1 tsp garam masala
2 tsp garlic and ginger paste
1 lb 9 oz/700 g skinless, boneless
    chicken breasts or thighs, diced
2 tbsp plain yogurt
2 tbsp chopped fresh cilantro,
    plus extra sprigs to garnish
2 fresh green chiles, seeded and
    finely chopped
2 tbsp lime juice
salt

method

1 Heat the ghee in a large heavy-bottom skillet. Add the onions and cook over low heat, stirring occasionally, for 10 minutes, or until golden. Add the tomatoes, nigella seeds, peppercorns, cardamom pods, cinnamon stick, chili powder, garam masala, and garlic and ginger paste, and season to taste with salt. Cook, stirring constantly, for 5 minutes.

2 Add the chicken and cook, stirring constantly, for 5 minutes, or until well coated in the spice paste. Stir in the yogurt. Cover and let simmer, stirring occasionally, for 10 minutes.

3 Stir in the chopped cilantro, chiles, and lime juice. Transfer to a warmed serving dish, garnish with cilantro sprigs, and serve immediately.

variation

Add 7 oz/200 g broccoli divided into very small florets and 3 oz/85 g small peas to the skillet, plus 2 fl oz/50 ml/ ¼ cup chicken stock, when the chicken has finished its initial cooking. Increase the simmering time to 12 minutes.

chicken tikka masala

ingredients

serves 4–6

14 oz/400 g canned chopped
    tomatoes
1¼ cups heavy cream
8 cooked tandoori chicken pieces
    (see page 28)
salt and pepper
fresh chopped cilantro, to garnish
cooked basmati rice, to serve

tikka masala

2 tbsp ghee or vegetable oil
1 large garlic clove, finely chopped
1 fresh red chile, seeded and
    chopped
2 tsp ground cumin
2 tsp ground paprika
½ tsp salt
pepper

method

1 To make the tikka masala, melt the ghee in a large skillet with a lid over medium heat. Add the garlic and chile and stir-fry for 1 minute. Stir in the cumin, paprika, and salt and pepper to taste and continue stirring for about 30 seconds.

2 Stir the tomatoes and cream into the skillet. Reduce the heat to low and let the sauce simmer for about 10 minutes, stirring frequently, until the liquid reduces and thickens.

3 Meanwhile, remove all the bones and any skin from the tandoori chicken pieces, then cut the meat into bite-size pieces.

4 Adjust the seasoning of the sauce, if necessary. Add the chicken pieces to the skillet, cover, and let simmer for 3–5 minutes, until the chicken is heated through. Garnish the dish with cilantro and serve with cooked basmati rice.

butter chicken

ingredients

serves 4–6

1 onion, chopped
1½ tbsp garlic and ginger paste
14 oz/400 g canned chopped
    tomatoes
¼–½ tsp chili powder
pinch of sugar
2 tbsp ghee or vegetable oil
½ cup water
1 tbsp tomato paste
3 tbsp butter, cut into small pieces
½ tsp garam masala
½ tsp ground cumin
½ tsp ground coriander
8 cooked tandoori chicken pieces
    (see page 28)
4 tbsp heavy cream
salt and pepper
chopped cashew nuts and fresh
    cilantro sprigs, to garnish

method

1 Put the onion and the garlic and ginger paste in a food processor, blender, or spice grinder and process until a paste forms. Add the tomatoes, chili powder, sugar, and a pinch of salt and process again until blended.

2 Melt the ghee in a wok or large skillet over medium–high heat. Add the tomato mixture and water and stir in the tomato paste.

3 Bring the mixture to a boil, stirring, then reduce the heat to very low and simmer for 5 minutes, stirring occasionally, until the sauce thickens.

4 Stir in half the butter, the garam masala, cumin, and coriander. Add the chicken pieces and stir until they are well coated. Simmer for about 10 minutes, or until the chicken is hot. Taste and adjust the seasoning, if necessary.

5 Lightly beat the cream in a small bowl and stir in several tablespoons of the hot sauce, beating continuously. Stir the cream mixture into the tomato sauce, then add the remaining butter and stir until it melts. Garnish with the chopped cashew nuts and cilantro sprigs and serve straight from the wok.

wok-cooked chicken in tomato & fenugreek sauce

ingredients

serves 4

1 lb 9 oz/700 g skinless, boneless
   chicken thighs, cut into
   1-inch/2.5-cm cubes
juice of 1 lime
1 tsp salt, or to taste
4 tbsp sunflower oil or olive oil
1 large onion, finely chopped
2 tsp ginger paste
2 tsp garlic paste
½ tsp ground turmeric
½–1 tsp chili powder
1 tbsp ground coriander
15 oz/425 g canned chopped
   tomatoes
½ cup warm water
1 tbsp dried fenugreek leaves
½ tsp garam masala
2 tbsp chopped fresh cilantro
   leaves
2–4 fresh green chiles
Indian bread, to serve

method

1 Place the chicken in a nonmetallic bowl and rub in the lime juice and salt. Cover and set aside for 30 minutes.

2 Heat the oil in a wok or heavy skillet over medium–high heat. Add the onion and stir-fry for 7–8 minutes, until it begins to color.

3 Add the ginger and garlic pastes and continue to stir-fry for about 1 minute. Add the turmeric, chili powder, and ground coriander, then reduce the heat slightly and cook the spices for 25–30 seconds. Add half the tomatoes, stir-fry for 3–4 minutes, and add the remaining tomatoes. Continue to cook, stirring, until the tomato juice has evaporated and the oil separates from the spice paste and floats on the surface.

4 Add the chicken and increase the heat to high. Stir-fry for 4–5 minutes, then add the warm water, reduce the heat to medium–low, and cook for 8–10 minutes, or until the sauce has thickened and the chicken is tender.

5 Add the fenugreek leaves, garam masala, half the cilantro leaves, and the chiles. Cook for 1–2 minutes, remove from the heat, and transfer to a serving plate. Garnish with the remaining cilantro and serve with Indian bread.

chicken with stir-fried spices

ingredients

serves 4

1 lb 9 oz/700 g skinless, boneless
     chicken breasts or thighs
juice of ½ lemon
1 tsp salt, or to taste
5 tbsp sunflower oil or olive oil
1 large onion, finely chopped
2 tsp garlic paste
2 tsp ginger paste
½ tsp ground turmeric
1 tsp ground cumin
2 tsp ground coriander
½–1 tsp chili powder
5½ oz/150 g canned chopped
     tomatoes
⅔ cup warm water
1 large garlic clove, finely chopped
1 small or ½ large red bell pepper,
     seeded and cut into
     1-inch/2.5-cm pieces
1 small or ½ large green bell
     pepper, seeded and cut into
     1-inch/2.5-cm pieces
1 tsp garam masala
Indian bread, to serve

method

1 Cut the chicken into 1-inch/2.5-cm cubes and put in a nonmetallic bowl. Add the lemon juice and salt and rub well into the chicken. Cover and let marinate in the refrigerator for 20 minutes.

2 Heat 4 tablespoons of the oil in a medium heavy-bottom saucepan over medium heat. Add the onion and cook, stirring frequently, for 8–9 minutes, until lightly browned. Add the garlic and ginger pastes and cook, stirring, for 3 minutes. Add the turmeric, cumin, coriander, and chili powder and cook, stirring, for 1 minute. Add the tomatoes and their juice and cook for 2–3 minutes, stirring frequently, until the oil separates from the spice paste.

3 Add the marinated chicken, increase the heat slightly, and cook, stirring, until it changes color. Add the warm water and bring to a boil. Reduce the heat, cover, and simmer for 25 minutes.

4 Heat the remaining 1 tablespoon of oil in a small saucepan or skillet over low heat. Add the garlic and cook, stirring frequently, until browned. Add the bell peppers, increase the heat to medium, and stir-fry for 2 minutes, then stir in the garam masala. Fold the bell pepper mixture into the curry. Remove from the heat and serve immediately with Indian bread.

cumin-scented chicken

ingredients

serves 4

1 lb 9 oz/700 g boneless chicken thighs or breasts, cut into 5-cm/2-inch pieces

juice of 1 lime

1 tsp salt, or to taste

3 tbsp sunflower oil or olive oil

1 tsp cumin seeds

1-inch/2.5-cm piece cinnamon stick

5 green cardamom pods, bruised

4 cloves

1 large onion, finely chopped

2 tsp garlic paste

2 tsp ginger paste

½ tsp ground turmeric

2 tsp ground cumin

½ tsp chili powder

8 oz/225 g canned chopped tomatoes

1 tbsp tomato paste

½ tsp sugar

1 cup warm water

½ tsp garam masala

2 tbsp chopped fresh cilantro leaves, plus extra sprigs to garnish

Indian bread, to serve

method

1 Put the chicken in a nonmetallic bowl and rub in the lime juice and salt. Cover and set aside for 30 minutes.

2 Heat the oil in a medium saucepan over low heat and add the cumin seeds, cinnamon, cardamom, and cloves. Let them sizzle for 25–30 seconds, then add the onion. Cook, stirring frequently, for 5 minutes, or until the onion has softened.

3 Add the garlic paste and ginger paste and cook for about 1 minute, then add the turmeric, ground cumin, and chili powder. Add the tomatoes, tomato paste, and sugar. Cook over medium heat, stirring frequently, until the tomatoes reach a pastelike consistency and the oil separates from the spice paste. Sprinkle over a little water if the mixture sticks to the pan.

4 Add the chicken and increase the heat to medium–high. Stir until the chicken changes color, then pour in the warm water. Bring to a boil, reduce the heat to medium–low, and cook for 12–15 minutes, or until the sauce has thickened and the chicken is tender.

5 Stir in the garam masala and chopped cilantro. Transfer to a serving dish and garnish with cilantro sprigs. Serve with Indian bread.

chicken biryani

ingredients

serves 8

1½ tsp finely chopped fresh ginger

1½ tsp crushed garlic

1 tbsp garam masala

1 tsp chili powder

2 tsp salt

1¼ cups plain yogurt

5 green cardamom pods, bruised

1 chicken, weighing
   3 lb 5 oz/1.5 kg

⅔ cup milk

1 tsp saffron strands

6 tbsp ghee or vegetable oil

2 onions, sliced

1 lb/450 g basmati rice

2 cinnamon sticks

4 fresh green chiles

4 tbsp lemon juice

2 tbsp cilantro leaves

method

1 Mix the ginger, garlic, garam masala, chili powder, half the salt, the yogurt, and the cardamom pods in a bowl. Skin and cut the chicken into 8 pieces, add to the spices, and mix well. Cover and marinate in the refrigerator for 3 hours.

2 Boil the milk in a small saucepan, sprinkle over the saffron, and set aside.

3 Heat the ghee in a saucepan. Add the onions and cook until golden. Transfer half of the onions and ghee to a bowl and set aside.

4 Place the rice and cinnamon sticks in a saucepan of water. Bring the rice to a boil and simmer for 4–5 minutes, then remove from the heat. Drain and place in a bowl. Mix with the remaining salt.

5 Chop the chiles and set aside. Add the chicken mixture to the pan containing the onions. Add half each of the chopped green chiles, lemon juice, cilantro, and saffron milk. Add the rice, then the rest of the ingredients, including the reserved onions and ghee. Cover tightly. Cook over low heat for 1 hour. Check that the meat is cooked through; if it is not cooked, return to the heat, and cook for 15 minutes. Mix well before serving.

tandoori chicken

ingredients

serves 4

4 chicken pieces, about
    8 oz/225 g each, skinned
juice of ½ lemon
½ tsp salt, or to taste
⅓ cup strained, whole-milk plain
    yogurt or Greek-style yogurt
3 tbsp heavy cream
1 tbsp chickpea flour
1 tbsp garlic paste
1 tbsp ginger paste
½–1 tsp chili powder
1 tsp ground coriander
½ tsp ground cumin
½ tsp garam masala
½ tsp ground turmeric
2 tbsp vegetable oil, for brushing
3 tbsp melted butter or olive oil
lemon wedges, to garnish
salad, to serve

method

1 Make 2–3 small incisions in each chicken piece and place in a large nonmetallic bowl. Rub in the lemon juice and salt, cover, and chill for 20 minutes.

2 Meanwhile, put the yogurt in a separate bowl and add the cream and chickpea flour. Beat with a fork until well blended and smooth. Add all the remaining ingredients, except the oil and melted butter, and mix thoroughly. Pour over the chicken and rub in well. Cover and chill in the refrigerator for 4–6 hours, or overnight. Return to room temperature before cooking.

3 Preheat the broiler to high. Line a broiler pan with foil and brush the rack with oil. Using tongs, lift the chicken pieces out of the marinade and put on the prepared rack, reserving the remaining marinade. Cook the chicken under the preheated broiler for 4 minutes on each side. Baste the chicken with the reserved marinade and cook for 2 minutes on each side.

4 Brush the chicken with the melted butter and cook for 5–6 minutes. Turn over and baste with the remaining marinade. Cook for 5–6 minutes, until the juices run clear when a skewer is inserted into the meat.

5 Transfer the chicken to a dish. Garnish with lemon wedges and serve with salad.

silky chicken kabobs

ingredients

serves 8

⅓ cup raw cashews
2 tbsp light cream
1 egg
1 lb/450 g skinless, boneless
   chicken breasts, coarsely
   chopped
½ tsp salt, or to taste
2 tsp garlic paste
2 tsp ginger paste
2 fresh green chiles, coarsely
   chopped (seeded if you like)
1 cup fresh cilantro, including the
   tender stalks, coarsely chopped
1 tsp garam masala
vegetable oil, for brushing
2 tbsp butter, melted
chutney, to serve

method

1 Put the cashews in a heatproof bowl, cover with boiling water, and let soak for 20 minutes. Drain and put in a food processor. Add the cream and egg and process the ingredients to a coarse mixture.

2 Add all the remaining ingredients, except the oil and melted butter, and process until smooth. Transfer to a bowl, cover, and let chill for 30 minutes.

3 Preheat the broiler to high. Brush the rack and 8 metal or presoaked wooden skewers lightly with oil. Have a bowl of cold water ready.

4 Divide the chilled mixture into 8 equal-size portions. Dip your hands into the bowl of cold water—this will stop the mixture from sticking to your fingers when you are molding it onto the skewers. Carefully mold each portion onto a skewer, forming it into a 6-inch/15-cm sausage shape. Arrange the kabobs on the prepared rack and cook for 4 minutes. Brush with half the melted butter and cook for 1 minute. Turn over and cook for 3 minutes. Baste with the remaining melted butter and cook for 2 minutes.

5 Remove from the heat and let the kabobs rest for 5 minutes before sliding them off the skewers with a knife. Serve with chutney.

meat

lamb dhansak

ingredients

serves 4–6

1 lb 9 oz/700 g boneless shoulder
    of lamb, trimmed and cut into
    2-inch/5-cm cubes
1 tsp salt, plus extra to taste
1 tbsp garlic and ginger paste
5 green cardamom pods
1 cup yellow lentils (toor dal)
3½ oz/100 g pumpkin, peeled,
    seeded, and chopped
1 carrot, thinly sliced
1 fresh green chile, seeded
    and chopped
1 tsp fenugreek powder
scant 2½ cups water
1 large onion, thinly sliced
2 tbsp ghee or vegetable oil
2 garlic cloves, crushed
chopped fresh cilantro, to garnish

dhansak masala
1 tsp garam masala
½ tsp ground coriander
½ tsp ground cumin
½ tsp chili powder
½ tsp ground turmeric
¼ tsp ground cardamom
¼ tsp ground cloves

method

1 Put the lamb and 1 teaspoon of salt in a large saucepan
with enough water to cover and bring to a boil. Reduce
the heat and simmer. Stir in the garlic and ginger paste
and cardamom pods and simmer for 30 minutes.

2 Meanwhile, put the lentils, pumpkin, carrot, chile, and
fenugreek powder in a large heavy-bottom saucepan
with water. Bring to a boil, stirring occasionally, then
reduce the heat and simmer until tender. Let cool
slightly, then pour it into a food processor or blender
and process until a thick, smooth sauce forms.

3 Put the onion in a bowl, sprinkle with 1 teaspoon of
salt, and let stand for about 5 minutes. Melt the ghee
in a flameproof casserole or large skillet with a
tight-fitting lid over high heat. Add the onion and
sauté, stirring, for 2 minutes. Remove one third of the
onion and continue sautéing the rest until golden
brown. Remove the fried onion from the pan.

4 Return the onion to the casserole with the garlic. Stir
in all the dhansak masala ingredients and cook for
2 minutes, stirring continuously. Add the cooked
lamb and stir. Add the lentil sauce and simmer over
medium heat to warm through, stirring and adding
a little extra water, if needed. Adjust the seasoning.
Sprinkle with the onion and garnish with cilantro.

lamb rogan josh

ingredients

serves 4

1½ cups plain yogurt

½ tsp ground asafetida, dissolved
   in 2 tbsp water

1 lb 9 oz/700 g boneless leg of
   lamb, trimmed and cut into
   2-inch/5-cm cubes

2 tomatoes, seeded and chopped

1 onion, chopped

2 tbsp ghee or vegetable oil

1½ tbsp garlic and ginger paste

2 tbsp tomato paste

2 bay leaves

1 tbsp ground coriander

¼–1 tsp chili powder, ideally
   Kashmiri chili powder

½ tsp ground turmeric

1 tsp salt

½ tsp garam masala

method

1 Put the yogurt in a large bowl and stir in the dissolved
   asafetida. Add the lamb and use your hands to rub in
   all the marinade, then set aside for 30 minutes.

2 Meanwhile, put the tomatoes and onion in a food
   processor or blender and process until blended. Melt
   the ghee in a flameproof casserole or large skillet with
   a tight-fitting lid. Add the garlic and ginger paste and
   stir until the aromas are released.

3 Stir in the tomato mixture, tomato paste, bay leaves,
   coriander, chili powder, and turmeric, reduce the
   heat to low, and simmer, stirring occasionally, for
   5–8 minutes.

4 Add the lamb and salt with any leftover marinade and
   stir for 2 minutes. Cover, reduce the heat to low, and
   simmer, stirring occasionally, for 30 minutes. The lamb
   should give off enough moisture to prevent it from
   catching on the bottom of the skillet, but if the sauce
   looks too dry, stir in a little water.

5 Sprinkle with the garam masala, re-cover the skillet,
   and continue simmering for 15–20 minutes, until the
   lamb is tender. Serve immediately.

lamb dopiaza

ingredients

serves 4

4 onions, sliced into rings
3 garlic cloves, coarsely chopped
1-inch/2.5-cm piece fresh ginger,
    grated
1 tsp ground coriander
1 tsp ground cumin
1 tsp chili powder
½ tsp ground turmeric
1 tsp ground cinnamon
1 tsp garam masala
4 tbsp water
5 tbsp butter or vegetable oil
1 lb 8 oz/680 g boneless lamb,
    cut into bite-size chunks
6 tbsp plain yogurt
salt and pepper
fresh cilantro leaves, to garnish
cooked basmati rice, to serve

method

1 Put half of the onion rings into a food processor with the garlic, ginger, ground coriander, cumin, chili powder, turmeric, cinnamon, and garam masala. Add the water and process to a paste.

2 Heat 4 tablespoons of the butter in a pan over medium heat. Add the remaining onions and cook, stirring, for 3 minutes. Remove from the heat. Lift out the onions with a slotted spoon and set aside. Heat the remaining butter in the pan over high heat, add the lamb, and cook, stirring, for 5 minutes. Lift out the meat and drain on paper towels.

3 Add the onion paste to the pan and cook over medium heat, stirring, until the oil separates. Stir in the yogurt, season to taste with salt and pepper, return the lamb to the pan, and stir well.

4 Bring the mixture gently to a boil, reduce the heat, cover, and simmer for 25 minutes. Stir in the reserved onion rings and cook for 5 minutes. Remove from the heat and garnish with cilantro leaves. Serve immediately with cooked basmati rice.

lamb pasanda

ingredients

serves 4–6

1 lb 5 oz/600 g boneless shoulder
   or leg of lamb
2 tbsp garlic and ginger paste
4 tbsp ghee or vegetable oil
3 large onions, chopped
1 fresh green chile, seeded
   and chopped
2 green cardamom pods, bruised
1 cinnamon stick, broken in half
2 tsp ground coriander
1 tsp ground cumin
1 tsp ground turmeric
generous 1 cup water
²/₃ cup heavy cream
4 tbsp ground almonds
1½ tsp salt
1 tsp garam masala
paprika and toasted slivered
   almonds, to garnish

method

1 Cut the meat into thin slices, then place the slices between plastic wrap and pound with a meat mallet. Put the lamb slices in a bowl, add the garlic and ginger paste, and rub well into the lamb. Cover and let marinate in the refrigerator for 2 hours.

2 Melt the ghee in a large skillet over medium–high heat. Add the onions and chile and sauté, stirring frequently, for 5–8 minutes, until golden brown.

3 Stir in the cardamom pods, cinnamon stick, ground coriander, cumin, and turmeric and continue stirring for 2 minutes, or until the spices are aromatic. Add the meat to the skillet and cook, stirring occasionally, for about 5 minutes, until it is browned on all sides and the fat begins to separate. Stir in the water and bring to a boil, still stirring. Reduce the heat to its lowest setting, cover the skillet tightly, and simmer for 40 minutes, or until the meat is tender.

4 Mix the cream and ground almonds together in a bowl. Beat in 6 tablespoons of the hot cooking liquid from the skillet, then gradually beat this mixture back into the skillet. Stir in the salt and garam masala. Simmer for 5 minutes, uncovered, stirring occasionally.

5 Garnish with a sprinkling of paprika and slivered almonds and serve.

lamb, tomato & eggplant curry

ingredients

serves 4

2 tbsp oil
1 lb 2 oz/500 g lamb fillet or leg,
   cut into cubes
1 large onion, coarsely chopped
2–3 tbsp Thai Red Curry Paste
1 eggplant, cut into small cubes
10 tomatoes, peeled, seeded,
   and coarsely chopped
14 fl oz/400 ml/1¾ cups
   coconut milk
10 fl oz/300 ml/1¼ cups
   lamb stock
2 tbsp chopped fresh cilantro,
   plus extra sprigs to garnish

method

1 Heat the oil in a large skillet. Add the lamb in batches and cook for 8–10 minutes, or until browned all over. Remove with a slotted spoon and set aside.

2 Add the onion to the skillet and cook for 2–3 minutes, or until just softened. Add the curry paste and stir-fry for 2 minutes. Add the eggplant, three-quarters of the tomatoes, and the lamb and stir together.

3 Add the coconut milk and stock and let simmer gently for 30–40 minutes, until the lamb is tender and the curry has thickened.

4 Mix the remaining tomatoes and chopped cilantro together in a small bowl, then stir into the curry. Serve immediately, garnished with cilantro sprigs.

peshawar-style lamb curry

ingredients

serves 4

4 tbsp sunflower oil or olive oil

1-inch/2.5-cm piece cinnamon stick

5 green cardamom pods, bruised

5 cloves

2 bay leaves

1 lb 9 oz/700 g boneless leg of lamb, cut into 1-inch/2.5-cm cubes

1 large onion, finely chopped

2 tsp garlic paste

2 tsp ginger paste

1 tbsp tomato paste

1 tsp ground turmeric

1 tsp ground coriander

1 tsp ground cumin

generous ½ cup thick plain yogurt

2 tsp chickpea flour or cornstarch

½–1 tsp chili powder

⅔ cup warm water

1 tbsp chopped fresh mint leaves

2 tbsp chopped fresh cilantro leaves

Indian bread, to serve

method

1 In a medium saucepan, heat the oil over low heat and add the cinnamon, cardamom, cloves, and bay leaves. Let them sizzle for 25–30 seconds, then add the meat, increase the heat to medium–high, and cook until the meat begins to brown and all the natural juices have evaporated.

2 Add the onion and garlic and ginger pastes and cook for 5–6 minutes, stirring frequently, then add the tomato paste, turmeric, coriander, and cumin. Continue to cook for 3–4 minutes.

3 Whisk together the yogurt, chickpea flour, and chili powder and add to the meat. Reduce the heat to low, add the warm water, cover, and simmer, stirring frequently to make sure that the sauce does not stick to the bottom of the pan, for 45–50 minutes, until the meat is tender. Simmer, uncovered, if necessary to thicken the sauce to the desired consistency.

4 Stir in the fresh mint and cilantro, remove from the heat, and serve with Indian bread.

lean lamb cooked in spinach

ingredients

serves 2–4

1¼ cups vegetable oil
2 onions, sliced
¼ bunch of fresh cilantro
2 fresh green chiles, chopped
1½ tsp finely chopped fresh ginger
1½ tsp crushed fresh garlic
1 tsp chili powder
½ tsp ground turmeric
1 lb/450 g lean lamb, cut into
    bite-size chunks
1 tsp salt
2 lb 4 oz/1 kg fresh spinach,
    trimmed, washed, and
    chopped
1¼ pints/700 ml/3 cups water
1 fresh red chile, finely chopped,
    to garnish

method

1 Heat the oil in a large, heavy-bottom skillet. Add the onions and cook until light golden.

2 Add the fresh cilantro and green chiles to the skillet and stir-fry for 3–5 minutes. Reduce the heat and add the ginger, garlic, chili powder, and turmeric, stirring the mixture well.

3 Add the lamb to the skillet and stir-fry for 5 minutes. Add the salt and the spinach and cook, stirring occasionally with a wooden spoon, for 3–5 minutes.

4 Add the water, stirring, and cook over low heat, covered, for 45 minutes. Remove the lid and check the meat. If it is not tender, turn the meat over, increase the heat, and cook, uncovered, until the surplus water has been absorbed. Stir-fry the mixture for 5–7 minutes.

5 Transfer the lamb and spinach mixture to a warmed serving dish and garnish with chopped red chile. Serve hot.

meatballs in creamy cashew nut sauce

ingredients

serves 4

1 lb/450 g fresh lean ground lamb
1 tbsp thick plain yogurt
1 large egg, beaten
½ tsp ground cardamom
½ tsp ground nutmeg
½ tsp pepper
½ tsp dried mint
½ tsp salt, or to taste
1¼ cups water
1-inch/2.5-cm piece cinnamon
   stick
5 green cardamom pods
5 cloves
2 bay leaves
3 tbsp sunflower oil or olive oil
1 onion, finely chopped
2 tsp garlic paste
1 tsp ground ginger
1 tsp ground fennel seeds
½ tsp ground turmeric
½–1 tsp chili powder
generous 1 cup cashews
⅔ cup heavy cream
1 tbsp crushed pistachios,
   to garnish

method

1 Put the lamb into a bowl and add the yogurt, egg, cardamom, nutmeg, pepper, mint, and salt. Knead the meat until it is smooth and velvety. Chill for 30–40 minutes, then divide into quarters. Make five balls out of each quarter and make them smooth and neat.

2 Bring the cold water to a boil in a large saucepan and add all the whole spices and the bay leaves. Add the meatballs in a single layer, reduce the heat to medium, cover the pan, and cook for 12–15 minutes. Remove the meatballs, cover, and keep hot. Strain the spiced stock and set aside.

3 Wipe out the pan and add the oil. Place over medium heat and add the onion and garlic paste. Add the ground ginger, fennel, turmeric, and chili powder. Stir-fry for 2–3 minutes, then add the strained stock and meatballs. Bring to a boil, reduce the heat to low, cover, and simmer for 10–12 minutes.

4 Meanwhile, process the cashews to a paste in a blender and add to the meatball mixture along with the cream. Simmer for 5–6 minutes, then remove from the heat. Garnish with crushed pistachios and serve.

lamb kabobs

ingredients

serves 4

⅓ cup raw cashews
3 tbsp heavy cream
1 egg
1 tbsp chickpea flour
2 fresh green chiles, coarsely
　　chopped
2 shallots, coarsely chopped
1 lb/450 g fresh ground lamb
1 tsp salt, or to taste
2 tsp garlic paste
2 tsp ginger paste
1 tsp ground cumin
1 tsp garam masala
1 tbsp chopped fresh mint leaves
2 tbsp chopped fresh cilantro
　　leaves
½ red bell pepper, finely chopped
2 tbsp vegetable oil, for brushing
4 tbsp butter, melted
salad and chutney, to serve

method

1 Put the cashews in a heatproof bowl, cover with boiling water, and let soak for 20 minutes. Drain and put in a food processor. Add the cream and egg and process the ingredients to a coarse mixture.

2 Add all the remaining ingredients, except the herbs, red bell pepper, oil, and butter, and process until thoroughly mixed. Transfer the mixture to a large bowl. Add the herbs and red bell pepper and mix well. Cover and chill in the refrigerator for 30–40 minutes.

3 Preheat the broiler to high. Brush the rack and 8 metal skewers lightly with oil. Have a bowl of cold water ready. Divide the chilled mixture into 8 equal-size portions. Dip your hands into the bowl of cold water—this will stop the mixture from sticking to your fingers when you are molding it onto the skewer. Carefully mold each portion onto a skewer, forming it into a 6-inch/15-cm sausage shape. Arrange the kabobs on the prepared rack and cook for 4 minutes. Brush with half the melted butter and cook for a minute. Turn over and cook for 3 minutes. Baste with the remaining melted butter and cook for 2 minutes.

4 Remove from the heat and let the kabobs rest for 5 minutes before sliding them off the skewers with a knife. Serve with salad and chutney.

kashmiri lamb chops

ingredients

serves 4

8 lamb chops
1¼ cups whole milk
1 tbsp ginger paste
½ tsp pepper
pinch of saffron threads, pounded
1½ tsp ground fennel seeds
1 tsp ground cumin
½ tsp chili powder
4 cloves
1-inch/2.5-cm piece cinnamon
    stick
4 green cardamom pods, bruised
1 tsp salt, or to taste
½ tsp garam masala
1 tbsp fresh mint leaves, chopped,
    or ½ tsp dried mint
1 tbsp chopped fresh cilantro
    leaves
mixed leaf salad, for serving

method

1 Remove the rind from the chops. Bring enough water to cover the chops to a boil in a medium saucepan. Add the chops, return to a boil, and cook for 2–3 minutes. Drain the chops, rinse, and drain again.

2 Put the drained chops into a large nonstick saucepan and add all the remaining ingredients, except the garam masala and herbs. Put the saucepan over medium heat and stir until the milk begins to bubble. Reduce the heat to low, cover, and cook for 30 minutes, turning the chops occasionally.

3 Remove from the heat. Using tongs, lift the chops out of the saucepan and shake the cooking liquid back into the saucepan. Strain the liquid and return to the saucepan with the chops. Cook over medium heat, turning frequently, for 7–8 minutes, until the liquid has evaporated and the chops are browned.

4 Sprinkle the garam masala evenly over the chops and add the mint and cilantro. Stir and cook for 1 minute. Serve immediately with a mixed salad.

sesame lamb chops

ingredients

serves 4

12 lamb chops, such as blade or rib
corn oil, for brushing
1½ tbsp sesame seeds
pepper and lime wedges,
    to serve

marinade
4 tbsp plain yogurt
2 tbsp grated lemon rind
1½ tsp ground cumin
1½ tsp ground coriander
¼ tsp chili powder
salt

method

1 To make the marinade, put the yogurt, lemon rind, cumin, coriander, chili powder, and salt to taste in a large bowl and stir together.

2 Use a sharp knife to trim any fat from the edge of the lamb chops and scrape the meat away from the long piece of bone. Using a rolling pin or the end of a large chef's knife, pound each chop until it is about ¼ inch/5 mm thick.

3 Add the chops to the bowl and use your hands to stir around until they are coated in the marinade. Let marinate for 20 minutes at room temperature, or cover the bowl and refrigerate for up to 4 hours. Return to room temperature before cooking.

4 Preheat the broiler to high and brush the broiler rack lightly with oil.

5 Arrange the chops on the broiler rack in a single layer, then sprinkle the sesame seeds over each. Broil the chops for about 7 minutes, without turning, for medium.

6 Grind fresh pepper over the chops and serve with lime wedges for squeezing over.

marinated lamb brochettes

ingredients

serves 4

1 lb 9 oz/700 g boned leg of lamb,
    cut into 1-inch/2.5-cm cubes
2 tbsp vinegar
½ tsp salt, or to taste
1 tbsp garlic paste
1 tbsp ginger paste
½ cup strained, whole-milk plain
    yogurt or Greek-style yogurt
1 tbsp chickpea flour
1 tsp ground cumin
1 tsp garam masala
½–1 tsp chili powder
½ tsp ground turmeric
3 tbsp olive oil or sunflower oil,
    plus 1 tbsp for brushing
½ red bell pepper, cut into
    1-inch/2.5-cm pieces
½ green bell pepper, cut into
    1-inch/2.5-cm pieces
8 shallots, halved
4 tbsp butter, melted
lemon wedges, to serve

method

1 Put the meat in a large nonmetallic bowl and add the vinegar, salt, and garlic and ginger pastes. Mix together thoroughly, cover, and let marinate in the refrigerator for 30 minutes.

2 Put the yogurt and chickpea flour in a separate bowl and beat together with a fork until smooth. Add the cumin, garam masala, chili powder, turmeric, and oil and mix together thoroughly. Add the yogurt mixture to the marinated meat, then add the bell peppers and shallots and stir until well blended. Cover and let marinate in the refrigerator for 2–3 hours, or overnight. Return to room temperature before cooking.

3 Preheat the broiler to high. Line the broiler pan with a piece of foil. Brush the rack and 4 metal skewers with the oil. Thread the marinated lamb, bell peppers, and shallots alternately onto the prepared skewers. Place the skewers on the prepared rack and cook for 4 minutes. Brush generously with half the melted butter and cook for 2 minutes. Turn over and cook for 3–4 minutes. Brush with the remaining butter and cook for 2 minutes.

4 Balance the brochettes over a large saucepan or skillet and let rest for 5–6 minutes before sliding off the skewers with a knife. Serve with the lemon wedges.

balti beef

ingredients

serves 4–6

2 tbsp ghee or vegetable oil
1 large onion, chopped
2 garlic cloves, crushed
2 large red bell peppers, seeded
    and chopped
1 lb 5 oz/600 g boneless beef,
    such as sirloin, thinly sliced
fresh cilantro sprigs,
    to garnish
Indian bread, to serve

balti sauce

2 tbsp ghee or vegetable oil
2 large onions, chopped
1 tbsp garlic and ginger paste
14 oz/400 g canned chopped
    tomatoes
1 tsp ground paprika
½ tsp ground turmeric
½ tsp ground cumin
½ tsp ground coriander
¼ tsp chili powder
¼ tsp ground cardamom
1 bay leaf
salt and pepper

method

1 To make the balti sauce, melt the ghee in a wok or large skillet over medium–high heat. Add the onions and garlic and ginger paste and stir-fry for about 5 minutes, until the onions are golden brown. Stir in the tomatoes, then add the paprika, turmeric, cumin, coriander, chili powder, cardamom, bay leaf, and salt and pepper to taste. Bring to a boil, stirring, then reduce the heat and simmer for 20 minutes, stirring occasionally.

2 Let the sauce cool slightly, then remove the bay leaf and pour the mixture into a food processor or blender and process to a smooth sauce.

3 Wipe out the wok and return it to medium–high heat. Add the ghee and melt. Add the onion and garlic and stir-fry for 5–8 minutes, until golden brown. Add the bell peppers and continue stir-frying for 2 minutes.

4 Stir in the beef and continue stirring for 2 minutes, until it starts to turn brown. Add the balti sauce and bring to a boil. Reduce the heat and simmer for 5 minutes, or until the sauce slightly reduces again and the bell peppers are tender. Adjust the seasoning, if necessary. Garnish with cilantro sprigs and serve with Indian bread.

beef madras

ingredients

serves 4–6

1–2 dried red chiles
2 tsp ground coriander
2 tsp ground turmeric
1 tsp black mustard seeds
½ tsp ground ginger
¼ tsp pepper
1¼ cups coconut cream
4 tbsp ghee or vegetable oil
2 onions, chopped
3 large garlic cloves, chopped
1 lb 9 oz/700 g lean braising beef,
    trimmed and cut into
    2-inch/5-cm cubes
generous 1 cup beef stock, plus
    a little extra if necessary
lemon juice
salt
pappadams, to serve

method

1 Depending on how hot you want this dish to be, chop the chiles with or without any seeds. The more seeds you include, the hotter the dish will be. Put the chopped chiles and any seeds in a small bowl with the coriander, turmeric, mustard seeds, ginger, and pepper and stir in a little of the coconut cream to make a thin paste.

2 Melt the ghee in a flameproof casserole or large skillet with a tight-fitting lid over medium–high heat. Add the onions and garlic and cook for 5–8 minutes, stirring frequently, until the onions are golden brown. Add the spice paste and stir for 2 minutes, or until you can smell the aromas.

3 Add the meat and stock and bring to a boil. Reduce the heat to its lowest level, cover tightly, and simmer for 1½ hours, or until the beef is tender. Check occasionally that the meat isn't catching on the bottom of the casserole, and stir in a little extra water or stock, if necessary.

4 Uncover the casserole and stir in the remaining coconut cream with the lemon juice and salt to taste. Bring to a boil, stirring, then reduce the heat again and simmer, still uncovered, until the sauce reduces slightly. Serve with pappadams.

beef korma with almonds

ingredients

serves 6

1¼ cups vegetable oil
3 onions, finely chopped
2 lb 4 oz/1 kg lean beef, cubed
1½ tsp garam masala
1½ tsp ground coriander
1½ tsp finely chopped fresh ginger
1½ tsp crushed garlic
1 tsp salt
⅔ cup plain yogurt
2 whole cloves
3 green cardamom pods
4 black peppercorns
2½ cups water
chapatis, to serve

to garnish

chopped blanched almonds
sliced fresh green chiles
chopped fresh cilantro

method

1 Heat the oil in a large heavy-bottom skillet. Add the onions and stir-fry for 8–10 minutes, until golden. Remove half of the onions and set aside.

2 Add the meat to the remaining onions in the skillet and stir-fry for 5 minutes. Remove the skillet from the heat.

3 Mix the garam masala, coriander, ginger, garlic, salt, and yogurt together in a large bowl. Gradually add the meat to the yogurt-and-spice mixture and mix to coat the meat on all sides. Place the meat mixture in the skillet, return to the heat, and stir-fry for 5–7 minutes, or until the mixture is nearly brown.

4 Add the cloves, cardamom pods, and peppercorns. Add the water, reduce the heat, cover, and let simmer for 45–60 minutes. If the water has completely evaporated but the meat is still not tender enough, add another 1¼ cups water and cook for 10–15 minutes, stirring occasionally.

5 Transfer to warmed serving dishes and garnish with the reserved onions, chopped almonds, chiles, and fresh cilantro. Serve with chapatis.

pork vindaloo

ingredients

serves 4

2–6 dried red chiles, torn
5 cloves
1-inch/2.5-cm piece cinnamon
    stick, broken up
4 green cardamom pods
½ tsp black peppercorns
½ mace blade
¼ nutmeg, lightly crushed
1 tsp cumin seeds
1½ tsp coriander seeds
½ tsp fenugreek seeds
2 tsp garlic paste
1 tbsp ginger paste
3 tbsp white wine vinegar
1 tbsp tamarind juice or juice
    of ½ lime
1 lb 9 oz/700 g boneless leg
    of pork, cut into 1-inch/
    2.5-cm cubes
4 tbsp olive oil, plus 2 tsp
2 large onions, finely chopped
generous 1 cup warm water,
    plus 4 tbsp
1 tsp salt, or to taste
1 tsp dark brown sugar
2 large garlic cloves, finely sliced
8–10 fresh or dried curry leaves

method

1 Grind the first ten ingredients (all the spices) to a fine powder in a spice grinder. Transfer the ground spices to a bowl and add the garlic and ginger pastes, vinegar, and tamarind juice. Mix together to form a paste.

2 Put the pork in a large nonmetallic bowl and rub about one-quarter of the spice paste into the meat. Cover and let marinate in the refrigerator for 30–40 minutes.

3 Heat the 4 tablespoons of oil in a heavy-bottom saucepan over medium heat, add the onions, and cook, stirring frequently, for 8–10 minutes, until lightly browned. Add the remaining spice paste and cook, for 5–6 minutes. Add 2 tablespoons of the warm water and cook until it evaporates. Repeat with the other 2 tablespoons of warm water.

4 Add the marinated pork and cook over medium–high heat until the meat changes color. Add the salt, sugar, and 1 cup of warm water. Bring to a boil, then reduce the heat to low, cover, and simmer for 50–55 minutes.

5 Meanwhile, heat the 2 teaspoons of oil in a small saucepan over low heat. Add the sliced garlic and cook, stirring, until it begins to brown. Add the curry leaves and let sizzle for 15–20 seconds. Stir the garlic mixture into the vindaloo. Remove from the heat and serve immediately.

pork with cinnamon & fenugreek

ingredients

serves 4

1 tsp ground coriander
1 tsp ground cumin
1 tsp chili powder
1 tbsp dried fenugreek leaves
1 tsp ground fenugreek
5 fl oz/150 ml/²/₃ cup plain yogurt
1 lb/450 g pork tenderloin, diced
4 tbsp ghee or vegetable oil
1 large onion, sliced
2-inch/5-cm piece fresh ginger,
    finely chopped
4 garlic cloves, finely chopped
1 cinnamon stick
6 green cardamom pods
6 whole cloves
2 bay leaves
175 ml/6 fl oz/³/₄ cup water
salt

method

1 Mix the coriander, cumin, chili powder, dried fenugreek, ground fenugreek, and yogurt together in a small bowl. Place the pork in a large, shallow nonmetallic dish and add the spice mixture, turning well to coat. Cover with plastic wrap and let marinate in the refrigerator for 30 minutes.

2 Melt the ghee in a large heavy-bottom saucepan. Cook the onion over low heat, stirring occasionally, for 5 minutes, or until softened. Add the ginger, garlic, cinnamon stick, cardamom pods, cloves, and bay leaves and cook, stirring continuously, for 2 minutes, or until the spices give off their aroma. Add the meat with its marinade and the water, and season to taste with salt. Bring to a boil, reduce the heat, cover, and let simmer for 30 minutes.

3 Transfer the meat mixture to a preheated wok or large heavy-bottom skillet and cook over low heat, stirring continuously, until dry and tender. If necessary, sprinkle occasionally with a little water to prevent the mixture from sticking to the wok. Serve immediately.

red curry pork with peppers

ingredients

serves 4

2 tbsp vegetable or peanut oil
1 onion, coarsely chopped
2 garlic cloves, chopped
1 lb/450 g pork tenderloin,
    thickly sliced
1 red bell pepper, seeded and
    cut into squares
6 oz/175 g button mushrooms,
    quartered
2 tbsp Thai Red Curry Paste
4 oz/115g/2½ cups coconut cream
1 tsp pork or vegetable bouillon
    powder
2 tbsp Thai soy sauce
4 tomatoes, peeled, seeded,
    and chopped
handful of fresh cilantro, chopped

method

1 Heat the oil in a wok or large skillet and sauté the onion and garlic for 1–2 minutes, until they are softened but not browned.

2 Add the pork slices and stir-fry for 2–3 minutes until browned all over. Add the bell pepper, mushrooms, and curry paste.

3 Add the coconut cream to the wok with the bouillon powder and soy sauce. Bring to a boil and let simmer for 4–5 minutes until the liquid has reduced and thickened.

4 Add the tomatoes and cilantro and cook for 1–2 minutes before serving.

variation

Replace the mushrooms with 1 medium zucchini, thinly sliced.

railway pork & vegetables

ingredients

serves 4–6

3 tbsp ghee or vegetable oil
1 large onion, finely chopped
4 green cardamom pods
3 cloves
1 cinnamon stick
1 tbsp garlic and ginger paste
2 tsp garam masala
¼–½ tsp chili powder
½ tsp ground asafetida
2 tsp salt, or to taste
1 lb 5 oz/600 g lean ground pork
1 potato, scrubbed and cut into
    ¼-inch/5-mm dice
14 oz/400 g canned chopped
    tomatoes
½ cup water
1 bay leaf
1 large carrot, coarsely grated
salt and pepper

method

1 Melt the ghee in a flameproof casserole or large skillet with a tight-fitting lid over medium heat. Add the onion and sauté, stirring occasionally, for 5–8 minutes, until golden brown. Add the cardamom pods, cloves, and cinnamon stick and continue sautéing, stirring, for 1 minute, or until you can smell the aromas.

2 Add the garlic and ginger paste, garam masala, chili powder, asafetida, and salt and stir for a minute. Add the pork and cook for 5 minutes, or until no longer pink, using a wooden spoon to break up the meat.

3 Add the potato, tomatoes, water, and bay leaf and bring to a boil, stirring. Reduce the heat to the lowest level, cover tightly, and simmer for 15 minutes. Stir in the carrot and simmer for 5 minutes, or until the potato and carrot are tender. Taste and adjust the seasoning, adding salt and pepper if necessary, and serve.

fish & seafood

bengali-style fish

ingredients

serves 4–6

1 tsp ground turmeric

1 tsp salt

2 lb 4 oz/1 kg monkfish or
cod fillet, skinned and
cut into pieces

6 tbsp mustard oil

4 fresh green chiles

1 tsp finely chopped fresh ginger

1 tsp crushed garlic

2 onions, finely chopped

2 tomatoes, finely chopped

2 cups water

chopped fresh cilantro, to garnish

Indian bread, to serve

method

1 Mix the turmeric and salt together in a small bowl,
then spoon the mixture over the fish pieces.

2 Heat the mustard oil in a large heavy-bottom skillet.
Add the fish and cook until pale yellow. Remove the
fish with a slotted spoon and set aside.

3 Place the chiles, ginger, garlic, onions, and tomatoes
in a mortar and grind with a pestle to make a paste.
Alternatively, place the ingredients in a food processor
and process until smooth.

4 Transfer the spice paste to a clean skillet and dry-fry
until golden brown.

5 Remove the skillet from the heat and place the fish
pieces in the paste without breaking up the fish.
Return the skillet to the heat, add the water, and cook
over medium heat for 15–20 minutes. Transfer to a
warmed serving dish, garnish with chopped cilantro,
and serve with Indian bread.

steamed fish with cilantro chutney

ingredients

serves 4

1 quantity of cilantro chutney
  (page 180)
1 large fresh banana leaf
vegetable oil or peanut oil,
  for brushing
4 white fish fillets, such as
  butterfish or sole, about
  5 oz/140 g each
salt and pepper
lime or lemon wedges, to serve

method

1 Prepare the cilantro chutney at least 2 hours in advance to let the flavors blend.

2 Meanwhile, cut the banana leaf into 4 squares large enough to fold comfortably around the fish to make tight pockets. Working with one piece of leaf at a time, very lightly rub the bottom with oil. Put one of the fish fillets in the center of the oiled side, flesh-side up. Spread one quarter of the cilantro chutney over the top and season to taste with salt and pepper.

3 Fold one side of the leaf over the fish, then fold the opposite side over. Turn the leaf so the folded edges are top and bottom. Fold the right-hand end of the leaf pocket into the center, then fold over the left-hand side. Close the leaf pocket. Repeat with the remaining ingredients and banana leaf squares.

4 Place a steamer large enough to hold the pockets in a single layer over a pan of boiling water. Add the fish, cover the pan, and steam for 15 minutes. Make sure the fish is cooked through and flakes easily. Serve the fish pockets with lime wedges.

butterfish in chili yogurt

ingredients

serves 4

2 tbsp vegetable oil or peanut oil
1 large onion, sliced
1½-inch/4-cm piece fresh ginger,
   finely chopped
½ tsp salt
¼ tsp ground turmeric
pinch of ground cinnamon
pinch of ground cloves
7 fl oz/200 ml/generous ¾ cup
   plain yogurt
1 tbsp all-purpose flour
small pinch of chili powder
4 skinless butterfish fillets, about
   5½ oz/150 g each, wiped dry
2 tbsp ghee or vegetable oil
salt and pepper
2 fresh fat green chiles, seeded
   and finely chopped, to garnish

method

1 Heat the oil in a large skillet over medium–high heat. Add the onion and sauté, stirring, for 8 minutes, or until it is soft and dark golden brown. Add the ginger and cook for a minute.

2 Stir in the salt, turmeric, cinnamon, and cloves and continue stirring for 30 seconds. Remove the pan from the heat and stir in the yogurt, a little at a time, beating constantly.

3 Transfer the yogurt mixture to a food processor or blender and process until a paste forms.

4 Season the flour with chili powder and salt and pepper to taste. Place it on a plate and lightly dust the fish fillets on both sides.

5 Melt the ghee in the wiped pan over medium–high heat. When it is bubbling, reduce the heat to medium and add the fish fillets in a single layer. Pan-fry for 2½ minutes, or until golden, then turn them over.

6 Continue cooking for a minute, then return the yogurt sauce to the pan and reheat, stirring. When the fillets flake easily and are cooked through and the sauce is hot, transfer to plates and sprinkle with the green chiles.

balti fish curry

ingredients

serves 4–6

2 lb/900 g thick whitefish fillets,
  rinsed and cut into large
  chunks
2 bay leaves, torn
⅔ cup ghee or vegetable oil
2 large onions, chopped
½ tbsp salt
⅔ cup water
chopped fresh cilantro,
  to garnish
Indian bread, to serve

marinade

½ tbsp garlic and ginger paste
1 fresh green chile, seeded and
  chopped
1 tsp ground coriander
1 tsp ground cumin
½ tsp ground turmeric
¼–½ tsp chili powder
1 tbsp water
salt

method

1 To make the marinade, mix the garlic and ginger paste,
   chile, coriander, cumin, turmeric, and chili powder
   together with salt to taste in a large bowl. Gradually stir
   in the water to form a thin paste. Add the fish chunks
   and smear with the marinade. Tuck the bay leaves
   underneath, cover, and let marinate in the refrigerator
   for at least 30 minutes, or up to 4 hours.

2 Remove the fish from the refrigerator 15 minutes in
   advance of cooking. Melt the ghee in a wok or large
   skillet over medium–high heat. Add the onions,
   sprinkle with the salt, and sauté, stirring frequently,
   for 8 minutes, or until they are very soft and golden.

3 Gently add the fish with its marinade and the bay leaves
   to the wok and stir in the water. Bring to a boil, then
   immediately reduce the heat and cook the fish for 4–5
   minutes, spooning the sauce over the fish and carefully
   moving the chunks around, until they are cooked through
   and the flesh flakes easily. Garnish with cilantro and serve
   with Indian bread.

goan-style seafood curry

ingredients

serves 4–6

3 tbsp vegetable oil or peanut oil
1 tbsp black mustard seeds
12 fresh or 1 tbsp dried curry
    leaves
6 shallots, finely chopped
1 garlic clove, crushed
1 tsp ground turmeric
½ tsp ground coriander
¼–½ tsp chili powder
scant 3 cups coconut cream
1 lb 2 oz/500 g whitefish fillets,
    cut into large chunks
1 lb/450 g large raw shrimp,
    peeled and deveined
juice and finely grated rind
    of 1 lime
salt

method

1 Heat the oil in a wok or large skillet over high heat. Add the mustard seeds and stir them around for about 1 minute, or until they pop. Stir in the curry leaves.

2 Add the shallots and garlic and stir for about 5 minutes, or until the shallots are golden. Stir in the turmeric, coriander, and chili powder and continue stirring for about 30 seconds.

3 Add the coconut cream. Bring to a boil, then reduce the heat to medium and stir for about 2 minutes.

4 Reduce the heat to low, add the fish, and simmer for 1 minute, spooning the sauce over the fish and very gently spooning it around. Add the shrimp and continue to simmer for 4–5 minutes, until the fish flakes easily and the shrimp turn pink and curl.

5 Add half the lime juice, then taste and add more lime juice and salt to taste. Sprinkle with the lime rind and serve.

variation

Replace the mustard seeds with dry mustard powder. Add 2 teaspoons of mustard powder to the pan with the turmeric.

fish in tomato & chili sauce with fried onion

ingredients

serves 4

1 lb 9 oz/700 g tilapia fillets, cut into 2-inch/5-cm pieces
2 tbsp lemon juice
1 tsp salt, or to taste
1 tsp ground turmeric
4 tbsp sunflower oil or olive oil, plus extra for shallow-frying
2 tsp sugar
1 large onion, finely chopped
2 tsp ginger paste
2 tsp garlic paste
½ tsp ground fennel seeds
1 tsp ground coriander
½–1 tsp chili powder
6 oz/175 g canned chopped tomatoes
1¼ cups warm water
2–3 tbsp chopped fresh cilantro leaves
cooked basmati rice, to serve

method

1 Lay the fish on a plate and gently rub in the lemon juice, half the salt, and half the turmeric. Set aside for 15–20 minutes. Pour enough oil to cover the bottom of a skillet to a depth of about ½ inch/1 cm and place over medium–high heat. When the oil is hot, fry the fish until well browned on both sides. Drain.

2 Heat the 4 tablespoons of oil in a medium saucepan over medium heat and add the sugar. Allow it to brown, without blackening. Add the onion and cook for 5 minutes, until softened. Add the ginger and garlic pastes and cook for 3–4 minutes.

3 Add the ground fennel seeds, coriander, chili powder, and the remaining turmeric. Cook for 1 minute, then add half the tomatoes. Cook until the tomato juice has evaporated, then add the remaining tomatoes. Cook, stirring, until the oil separates from the spice paste.

4 Pour in the warm water and add the remaining salt. Bring to a boil, then add the fish, stir gently, and reduce the heat to low. Cook, uncovered, for 5–6 minutes, then stir in half the cilantro leaves and remove from the heat. Sprinkle with the remaining cilantro and serve with cooked basmati rice.

fish korma

ingredients

serves 4

1 lb 9 oz/700 g tilapia fillets,
    cut into 2-inch/5-cm pieces
1 tbsp lemon juice
1 tsp salt
1/2 cup raw unsalted cashews
3 tbsp sunflower oil or olive oil
2-inch/5-cm piece cinnamon stick,
    halved
4 green cardamom pods, bruised
2 cloves
1 large onion, finely chopped
1–2 fresh green chiles, chopped
    (seeded if you like)
2 tsp ginger paste
2 tsp garlic paste
2/3 cup light cream
1/4 cup plain yogurt
1/4 tsp ground turmeric
1/2 tsp sugar
1 tbsp toasted slivered almonds,
    to garnish
Indian bread, to serve

method

1 Place the fish on a large plate and gently rub in the lemon juice and 1/2 teaspoon of the salt. Set aside for 20 minutes. Put the cashews in a bowl, cover with boiling water, and let soak for 15 minutes.

2 Heat the oil in a wide shallow saucepan over low heat and add the cinnamon, cardamom, and cloves. Let them sizzle for 30–40 seconds.

3 Add the onion, chiles, ginger paste, and garlic paste. Increase the heat slightly and cook, stirring frequently, for 9–10 minutes, until the onion is very soft.

4 Meanwhile, drain the cashews and process them with the cream and yogurt.

5 Stir the turmeric into the onion mixture and add the processed ingredients, the remaining salt, and the sugar. Mix thoroughly and arrange the fish in the sauce in a single layer. Bring to a slow simmer, cover the pan, and cook for 5 minutes. Remove the lid and shake the pan gently from side to side. Spoon some of the sauce over the pieces of fish. Re-cover and cook for 3–4 minutes.

6 Transfer to a serving dish and garnish with the slivered almonds. Serve with Indian bread.

fish tikka

ingredients

serves 4

pinch of saffron threads, pounded
1 tbsp hot milk
⅓ cup strained, whole-milk
     plain yogurt
1 tbsp garlic paste
1 tbsp ginger paste
.1 tsp salt, or to taste
½ tsp granulated sugar
juice of ½ lemon
½–1 tsp chili powder
½ tsp garam masala
1 tsp ground fennel seeds
2 tsp chickpea flour
1 lb 10 oz/750 g salmon fillets,
     skinned and cut into
     2-inch/5-cm cubes
3 tbsp olive oil, plus extra
     for brushing
sliced tomatoes and cucumber,
     to garnish
lemon wedges, to serve

method

1 Soak the pounded saffron in the hot milk for
10 minutes.

2 Put all the remaining ingredients, except the fish and
oil, in a bowl and beat with a fork or a wire whisk until
smooth. Stir in the saffron and milk, mix well, and add
the fish cubes. Using a metal spoon, mix gently, turning
the fish around until fully coated with the marinade.
Cover and let marinate in the refrigerator for 2 hours.
Return to room temperature before cooking.

3 Preheat the broiler to high. Brush the rack generously
with oil and 8 metal skewers lightly with oil. Line the
broiler pan with a piece of foil.

4 Thread the fish cubes onto the prepared skewers,
leaving a narrow gap between each piece. Arrange
on the prepared rack and cook for 3 minutes. Brush
half the 3 tablespoons of oil over the kabobs and cook
for a minute. Turn over and brush any remaining
marinade over the fish. Cook for 3 minutes. Brush the
remaining oil over the fish and cook for 2 minutes,
or until the fish is lightly charred.

5 Remove from the heat and let rest for 5 minutes.
Garnish with tomatoes and cucumber and serve
with lemon wedges for squeezing over.

mussels with mustard seeds & shallots

ingredients

serves 4

4 lb 8 oz/2 kg mussels, scrubbed
  and debearded
3 tbsp vegetable oil or peanut oil
1/2 tbsp black mustard seeds
8 shallots, chopped
2 garlic cloves, crushed
2 tbsp distilled white vinegar
4 small fresh red chiles
1 1/4 cups coconut cream
10 fresh or 1 tbsp dried
  curry leaves
1/2 tsp ground turmeric
1/4–1/2 tsp chili powder
salt

method

1 Discard any mussels with broken shells and any that refuse to close when tapped with a knife. Set aside.

2 Heat the oil in a wok or large skillet over medium–high heat. Add the mustard seeds and stir them around for 1 minute, or until they start to pop.

3 Add the shallots and garlic and cook, stirring frequently, for 3 minutes, or until they start to brown. Stir in the vinegar, whole chiles, coconut cream, curry leaves, turmeric, chili powder, and a pinch of salt and bring to a boil, stirring.

4 Reduce the heat to very low. Add the mussels, cover the wok, and let the mussels simmer, shaking the wok frequently, for 3–4 minutes, or until they are all open. Discard any mussels that remain closed. Ladle the mussels into deep bowls, then taste the broth and add extra salt, if necessary. Spoon over the mussels and serve.

mussels in coconut sauce

ingredients

serves 4

2 lb 4 oz/1 kg mussels, scrubbed
    and debearded
3 tbsp ghee or vegetable oil
1 onion, finely chopped
1 tsp garlic paste
1 tsp ginger paste
1 tsp ground cumin
1 tsp ground coriander
½ tsp ground turmeric
pinch of salt
2½ cups canned coconut milk
chopped fresh cilantro,
    to garnish

method

1 Discard any mussels with broken shells and any that refuse to close when tapped with a knife. Set aside.

2 Heat the ghee in a large heavy-bottom skillet. Add the onion and cook over low heat, stirring occasionally, for 10 minutes, or until golden.

3 Add the garlic and ginger pastes and cook, stirring constantly, for 2 minutes. Add the cumin, ground coriander, turmeric, and salt and cook, stirring constantly, for 2 minutes. Stir in the coconut milk and bring to a boil.

4 Add the mussels, cover, and cook for 5 minutes, or until the mussels have opened. Discard any mussels that remain closed. Transfer the mussels, with the coconut sauce, to a large warmed serving dish. Sprinkle with chopped cilantro and serve immediately.

shrimp & pineapple tikka

ingredients

serves 4

1 tsp cumin seeds
1 tsp coriander seeds
½ tsp fennel seeds
½ tsp yellow mustard seeds
¼ tsp fenugreek seeds
¼ tsp nigella seeds
pinch of chili powder
2 tbsp lemon or pineapple juice
12 jumbo shrimp, peeled,
    deveined, and tails left intact
12 bite-size wedges of fresh or
    well-drained canned pineapple
salt
chopped fresh cilantro, to garnish

method

1 If you are using wooden skewers for this rather than metal ones, place 4 skewers upright in a tall glass of water to soak for 20 minutes so they do not burn under the broiler. Dry-roast the cumin, coriander, fennel, mustard, fenugreek, and nigella seeds in a hot skillet over high heat, stirring them around constantly, until you can smell the aroma of the spices. Immediately turn the spices out of the pan so they do not burn.

2 Put the spices in a spice grinder or mortar, add the chili powder and salt to taste, and grind to a fine powder. Transfer to a nonmetallic bowl and stir in the lemon juice.

3 Add the shrimp to the bowl and stir them around so they are well coated, then set aside to marinate for 10 minutes. Meanwhile, preheat the broiler to high.

4 Thread 3 shrimp and 3 pineapple wedges alternately onto each wooden or metal skewer. Broil about 4 inches/10 cm from the heat for 2 minutes on each side, brushing with any leftover marinade, until the shrimp turn pink and are cooked through.

5 Serve the shrimp and pineapple wedges on the skewers on a plate with plenty of cilantro sprinkled over the top.

shrimp pooris

ingredients

serves 6

2 tsp coriander seeds
½ tsp black peppercorns
1 large garlic clove, crushed
1 tsp ground turmeric
¼–½ tsp chili powder
½ tsp salt
3 tbsp ghee or vegetable oil
1 onion, grated
1 lb 12 oz/800 g canned
   crushed tomatoes
pinch of sugar
1 lb 2 oz/500 g small, cooked,
   peeled shrimp, thawed if frozen
½ tsp garam masala, plus extra
   to garnish
6 pooris, kept warm
chopped fresh cilantro, to garnish

method

1 Put the coriander seeds, peppercorns, garlic, turmeric, chili powder, and salt in a small food processor, spice grinder, or mortar and blend to a thick paste.

2 Melt the ghee in a wok or large skillet over medium–low heat. Add the paste and cook, stirring continuously, for about 30 seconds.

3 Add the grated onion and stir for 30 seconds. Stir in the tomatoes and the sugar. Bring to a boil, stirring, and let bubble for 10 minutes, mashing the tomatoes against the side of the wok to break them down, or until reduced. Taste and add extra salt, if necessary.

4 Add the shrimp and sprinkle with the garam masala. When the shrimp are hot, arrange the hot pooris on plates and top each one with a portion of the shrimp. Sprinkle with the cilantro and garam masala and serve.

shrimp in coconut milk with chiles & curry leaves

ingredients

serves 4

4 tbsp sunflower oil or olive oil
½ tsp black or brown mustard
   seeds
½ tsp fenugreek seeds
1 large onion, finely chopped
2 tsp garlic paste
2 tsp ginger paste
1–2 fresh green chiles, chopped
   (seeded if you like)
1 tbsp ground coriander
½ tsp ground turmeric
½ tsp chili powder
1 tsp salt, or to taste
generous 1 cup canned
   coconut milk
1 lb/450 g cooked, peeled jumbo
   shrimp, thawed and drained
   if frozen
1 tbsp tamarind juice
   or juice of ½ lime
½ tsp crushed black pepper
10–12 fresh or dried curry leaves

method

1 Heat 3 tablespoons of the oil in a medium saucepan over medium–high heat. When hot, but not smoking, add the mustard seeds, followed by the fenugreek seeds and the onion. Cook, stirring frequently, for 5–6 minutes, until the onion is softened but not browned. Add the garlic and ginger pastes and the chiles and cook, stirring frequently, for 5–6 minutes, until the onion is a light golden color.

2 Add the coriander, turmeric, and chili powder and cook, stirring, for 1 minute. Add the salt and coconut milk, followed by the shrimp and tamarind juice. Bring to a slow simmer and cook, stirring occasionally, for 3–4 minutes.

3 Meanwhile, heat the remaining oil in a very small saucepan over medium heat. Add the pepper and curry leaves. Turn off the heat and let sizzle for 20–25 seconds, then fold the aromatic oil into the shrimp mixture. Remove from the heat and serve immediately.

tandoori shrimp

ingredients

serves 4

4 tbsp plain yogurt
2 fresh green chiles, seeded
    and chopped
½ tbsp garlic and ginger paste
seeds from 4 green cardamom
    pods
2 tsp ground cumin
1 tsp tomato paste
¼ tsp ground turmeric
¼ tsp salt
pinch of chili powder, ideally
    Kashmiri chili powder
24 raw jumbo shrimp, thawed
    if frozen, peeled, deveined,
    and tails left intact
oil, for greasing
lemon or lime wedges, to serve

method

1 Put the yogurt, chiles, and garlic and ginger paste in a small food processor or spice grinder and process to a paste. Alternatively use a pestle and mortar. Transfer the paste to a large nonmetallic bowl and stir in the cardamom seeds, cumin, tomato paste, turmeric, salt, and chili powder.

2 Add the shrimp to the bowl and use your hands to make sure they are coated with the yogurt marinade. Cover the bowl with plastic wrap and chill for at least 30 minutes, or up to 4 hours.

3 When you are ready to cook, heat a large grill pan or skillet over high heat until a few drops of water "dance" when they hit the surface. Use crumpled paper towels or a pastry brush to grease the hot pan very lightly with oil.

4 Use tongs to lift the shrimp out of the marinade, letting the excess drip back into the bowl, then place the shrimp on the pan and cook for 2 minutes. Flip the shrimp over and cook for 1–2 minutes, until they turn pink, curl, and are opaque all the way through when you cut one. Serve the shrimp immediately with lemon or lime wedges for squeezing over.

vegetables & pulses

mushroom bhaji

ingredients

serves 4

10 oz/280 g button mushrooms
4 tbsp sunflower oil or olive oil
1 onion, finely chopped
1 fresh green chile, finely chopped
    (seeded if you like)
2 tsp garlic paste
1 tsp ground cumin
1 tsp ground coriander
½ tsp chili powder
½ tsp salt, or to taste
1 tbsp tomato paste
3 tbsp water
1 tbsp snipped fresh chives,
    to garnish

method

1 Wipe the mushrooms with damp paper towels and slice thickly.

2 Heat the oil in a medium saucepan over medium heat. Add the onion and chile and cook, stirring, for 5–6 minutes, until the onion is softened but not browned. Add the garlic paste and cook, stirring, for 2 minutes.

3 Add the cumin, coriander, and chili powder and cook, stirring, for 1 minute. Add the mushrooms, salt, and tomato paste and stir until all the ingredients are blended.

4 Sprinkle the water evenly over the mushrooms and reduce the heat to low. Cover and cook for 5 minutes, stir, then cook for an additional 5 minutes. The sauce should have thickened, but if it appears runny, cook, uncovered, for 3–4 minutes, or until you achieve the desired consistency.

5 Transfer to a serving dish, sprinkle the chives on top, and serve immediately.

vegetable korma

ingredients

serves 4

½ cup cashews, soaked in
　¾ cup boiling water
good pinch of saffron threads,
　soaked in 2 tbsp hot milk
1 head of cauliflower, divided into
　½-inch/1-cm florets
4 oz/115 g green beans, cut into
　1-inch/2.5-cm lengths
2 carrots, cut into 1-inch/
　2.5-cm sticks
4 tbsp sunflower oil or olive oil
1 large onion, finely chopped
2 tsp ginger paste
1–2 fresh green chiles, chopped
　(seeded if you like)
2 tsp ground coriander
½ tsp ground turmeric
6 tbsp warm water
1¾ cups vegetable stock
½ tsp salt, or to taste
9 oz/250 g young, waxy potatoes,
　boiled, cooled, and halved
2 tbsp light cream
2 tsp ghee or butter
1 tsp garam masala
¼ tsp grated nutmeg

method

1 Soak the cashew nuts and saffron threads. Blanch the vegetables in a saucepan of boiling salted water, then drain and immediately plunge in cold water. The cauliflower and green beans should each be blanched for 3 minutes; the carrots will need 4 minutes.

2 Heat the oil in a medium heavy-bottom saucepan over medium heat. Add the onion, ginger paste, and chiles and cook, stirring frequently, for 5–6 minutes, until the onion is softened. Add the coriander and turmeric and cook, stirring, for 1 minute. Add half the warm water and cook for 2–3 minutes. Repeat this process, then cook, stirring frequently, for 2–3 minutes, or until the oil separates from the spice paste.

3 Add the stock, saffron and milk mixture, and salt, and bring to a boil. Drain the vegetables, add to the saucepan with the potatoes, and return to a boil. Reduce the heat to low and simmer for 2–3 minutes. Meanwhile, put the cashews and their soaking water in a food processor and process until well blended. Add to the korma, then stir in the cream.

4 Melt the ghee in a small saucepan over low heat. Add the garam masala and nutmeg and sizzle gently for 20–25 seconds. Fold the spiced butter into the korma. Remove from the heat and serve.

cauliflower, eggplant & green bean korma

ingredients

serves 4–6

generous ½ cup cashews
1½ tbsp garlic and ginger paste
scant 1 cup water
4 tbsp ghee or vegetable oil
1 large onion, chopped
5 green cardamom pods, bruised
1 cinnamon stick, broken in half
¼ tsp ground turmeric
generous 1 cup heavy cream
5 oz/140 g new potatoes, scrubbed
    and chopped into ½-inch/
    1-cm pieces
1½ cups cauliflower florets
½ tsp garam masala
5 oz/140 g eggplant, chopped into
    1-inch/2.5-cm chunks
5 oz/140 g green beans, chopped
    into 1-inch/2.5-cm lengths
salt and pepper
chopped fresh mint, to garnish

method

1 Heat a large flameproof casserole over high heat. Add the cashews and stir them until they start to brown, then immediately turn them out of the casserole.

2 Put the nuts in a spice grinder with the garlic and ginger paste and 1 tablespoon of the water and process to a coarse paste.

3 Melt half the ghee in the casserole over medium–high heat. Add the onion and sauté for 5–8 minutes, until golden brown. Add the nut paste and stir for 5 minutes. Stir in the cardamom pods, cinnamon stick, and turmeric.

4 Add the cream and the remaining water and bring to a boil, stirring. Reduce the heat to very low, cover, and simmer for 5 minutes.

5 Add the potatoes, cauliflower, and garam masala and simmer, covered, for 5 minutes. Stir in the eggplant and green beans and simmer until all the vegetables are tender. Check the sauce occasionally to make sure it isn't sticking, and stir in a little water if needed.

6 Taste and add seasoning, if necessary. Sprinkle with the mint and serve.

cauliflower & sweet potato curry

ingredients

serves 4

4 tbsp ghee or vegetable oil
2 onions, finely chopped
1 tsp Bengali five-spice mix
1 head of cauliflower, broken
    into florets
12 oz/350 g sweet potatoes, diced
2 fresh green chiles, seeded and
    finely chopped
1 tsp ginger paste
2 tsp paprika
1½ tsp ground cumin
1 tsp ground turmeric
½ tsp chili powder
3 tomatoes, quartered
2 cups fresh or frozen peas
3 tbsp plain yogurt
1 cup vegetable stock or water
1 tsp garam masala
fresh cilantro sprigs, to garnish
salt

method

1 Heat the ghee in a large heavy-bottom skillet. Add the onions and Bengali five-spice mix and cook over low heat, stirring frequently, for 10 minutes, or until the onions are golden. Add the cauliflower, sweet potatoes, and chiles and cook, stirring frequently, for 3 minutes.

2 Stir in the ginger paste, paprika, cumin, turmeric, and chili powder and cook, stirring constantly, for 3 minutes. Add the tomatoes and peas and stir in the yogurt and stock. Season with salt to taste, cover, and let simmer for 20 minutes, or until the vegetables are tender.

3 Sprinkle over the garam masala and transfer to a warmed serving dish. Garnish with cilantro sprigs and serve immediately.

variation

Replace the peas with green beans, cut into small pieces.

cumin-scented eggplant & potato curry

Good, but spicy

ingredients

serves 4

1 large eggplant, about
   12 oz/350 g
8 oz/225 g potatoes, boiled
   in their skins and cooled
3 tbsp sunflower oil or olive oil
½ tsp black mustard seeds
½ tsp nigella seeds
½ tsp fennel seeds
1 onion, finely chopped
1-inch/2.5-cm piece fresh
   ginger, grated
2 fresh green chiles, chopped
   (seeded if you like)
½ tsp ground cumin
1 tsp ground coriander
1 tsp ground turmeric
½ tsp chili powder
1 tbsp tomato paste
scant 2 cups warm water
1 tsp salt, or to taste
½ tsp garam masala
2 tbsp chopped fresh
   cilantro leaves
Indian bread, to serve

method

1 Quarter the eggplant lengthwise and cut the stem end of each quarter into 2-inch/5-cm pieces. Halve the remaining part of the quarter and cut into 2-inch/5-cm pieces. Soak the eggplant pieces in cold water.

2 Peel the potatoes and cut into 2-inch/5-cm cubes. Set aside. Heat the oil in a large saucepan over medium heat. When hot, add the mustard seeds and, as soon as they start popping, add the nigella seeds and fennel seeds.

3 Add the onion, ginger, and chiles and cook for 7–8 minutes, until the mixture begins to brown. Add the cumin, coriander, turmeric, and chili powder. Cook for about 1 minute, then add the tomato paste. Cook for another minute, then pour in the warm water and add the salt and drained eggplant. Bring to a boil and cook over medium heat for 8–10 minutes, stirring frequently. At the start of cooking, the eggplant will float, but once it soaks up the liquid it will sink quickly. When the eggplant sinks, add the potatoes and cook for 2–3 minutes, stirring.

4 Stir in the garam masala and chopped cilantro and remove from the heat. Serve with Indian bread.

tofu & vegetable curry

ingredients

serves 4

vegetable or peanut oil,
 for deep-frying
8 oz/225 g firm tofu, drained
 and cut into cubes
2 tbsp vegetable or peanut oil
2 onions, chopped
2 garlic cloves, chopped
1 fresh red chile, seeded and sliced
3 celery stalks, diagonally sliced
8 oz/225 g mushrooms,
 thickly sliced
4 oz/115 g baby corn, cut in half
1 red bell pepper, seeded and
 cut into strips
3 tbsp Thai Red Curry Paste
1¾ cups coconut milk
1 tsp jaggery or soft light
 brown sugar
2 tbsp Thai soy sauce
5 cups baby spinach leaves

method

1 Heat the oil for deep-frying in a skillet and deep-fry the
 tofu cubes, in batches, for 4–5 minutes, until crisp and
 browned. Remove with a slotted spoon and drain on
 paper towels.

2 Heat 2 tablespoons of the oil in a skillet and stir-fry
 the onions, garlic, and chile for 1–2 minutes, until they
 start to soften. Add the celery, mushrooms, corn, and
 red bell pepper, and stir-fry for 3–4 minutes, until they
 soften.

3 Stir in the curry paste and coconut milk and gradually
 bring to a boil. Add the jaggery and soy sauce and
 then the spinach. Cook, stirring constantly, until the
 spinach has wilted. Serve immediately, topped with
 the tofu.

green bean & potato curry

ingredients

serves 6

1¼ cups vegetable oil
1 tsp white cumin seeds
1 tsp mixed mustard and
      onion seeds
4 dried red chiles
3 fresh tomatoes, sliced
1 tsp salt
1 tsp fresh ginger, finely chopped
1 tsp crushed fresh garlic
1 tsp chili powder
7 oz/200 g green beans, diagonally
      sliced into 1-inch/2.5-cm
      pieces
2 potatoes, peeled and diced
1¼ cups water
fresh cilantro, chopped and green
      chiles, finely sliced, to garnish

method

1 Heat the oil in a large, heavy-bottom pan. Add the white cumin seeds, mustard and onion seeds, and dried red chiles, stirring well.

2 Add the tomatoes to the pan and stir-fry the mixture for 3–5 minutes.

3 Mix the salt, ginger, garlic, and chili powder together in a bowl and spoon into the saucepan. Blend the whole mixture together.

4 Add the green beans and potatoes to the pan and stir-fry for 5 minutes.

5 Add the water to the pan, reduce the heat, and let simmer for 10–15 minutes, stirring occasionally. Transfer to a warmed serving dish, garnish with chopped cilantro and green chiles, and serve.

vegetable sambar

ingredients

serves 6

1 lb 12 oz/800 g canned tomatoes
2 tbsp dry unsweetened coconut
2 tbsp lemon juice
1 tbsp yellow mustard seeds
1½ oz/40 g/scant ¼ cup raw
　or brown sugar
2 tbsp ghee or vegetable oil
2 onions, sliced
4 cardamom pods, lightly crushed
6 curry leaves, plus extra to garnish
2 tsp ground coriander
2 tsp ground cumin
1 tsp ground turmeric
1 tsp ginger paste
7 oz/200 g/1 cup toor dalh
　(yellow lentils)
1 lb/450 g sweet potatoes,
　cut into chunks
2 lb/900 g potatoes, cut into
　chunks
2 carrots, sliced
2 zucchini, cut into chunks
1 eggplant, cut into chunks
salt

method

1 Place the tomatoes and their can juices, coconut, 1 tablespoon of the lemon juice, the mustard seeds, and sugar in a food processor or blender and process until smooth.

2 Heat the ghee in a large, heavy-bottom pan. Add the onion and cook over low heat, stirring occasionally, for 10 minutes, or until golden. Add the cardamoms, curry leaves, coriander, cumin, turmeric, and ginger paste and cook, stirring constantly, for 1–2 minutes, or until the spices give off their aroma.

3 Stir in the tomato mixture and dal and bring to a boil. Reduce the heat, cover, and let simmer for 10 minutes.

4 Add the sweet potatoes, potatoes, and carrots, re-cover the pan, and let simmer for an additional 15 minutes. Add the zucchini, eggplant, and remaining lemon juice, add salt to taste, re-cover, and let simmer for an additional 10–15 minutes, or until the vegetables are tender. Serve garnished with curry leaves.

okra stir-fried with onions

ingredients

serves 4

10 oz/280 g okra
1 small red bell pepper
1 onion
2 tbsp sunflower oil or olive oil
1 tsp black or brown mustard
    seeds
½ tsp cumin seeds
3 large garlic cloves, lightly
    crushed, then chopped
½ tsp chili powder
½ tsp salt, or to taste
½ tsp garam masala
cooked basmati rice, to serve

method

1 Scrub each okra gently, rinse well in cold running water, then slice off the hard head. Halve diagonally and set aside.

2 Remove the seeds and core from the red bell pepper and cut into 1½-inch/4-cm strips. Halve the onion lengthwise and cut into ¼-inch/5-mm thick slices.

3 Heat the oil in a heavy-bottom skillet or wok over medium heat. When hot, but not smoking, add the mustard seeds, followed by the cumin seeds. Remove from the heat and add the garlic. Return to low heat and cook the garlic gently, stirring, for 1 minute, or until lightly browned.

4 Add the okra, red bell pepper, and onion, increase the heat to medium–high, and stir-fry for 2 minutes. Add the chili powder and salt and stir-fry for 3 minutes. Add the garam masala and stir-fry for 1 minute. Remove from the heat and serve immediately with cooked basmati rice.

garlic & chile-flavored potatoes with cauliflower

ingredients

serves 4

12 oz/350 g young, waxy potatoes
1 head of cauliflower
2 tbsp sunflower oil or olive oil
1 tsp black or brown mustard
    seeds
1 tsp cumin seeds
5 large garlic cloves, lightly
    crushed, then chopped
1–2 fresh green chiles, finely
    chopped (seeded if
    you like)
½ tsp ground turmeric
½ tsp salt, or to taste
2 tbsp chopped fresh cilantro
    leaves

method

1 Cook the potatoes in their skins in a saucepan of boiling water for 20 minutes, or until tender. Drain, then soak in cold water for 30 minutes. Peel them, if you like, then halve or quarter according to their size—they should be only slightly bigger than the size of the cauliflower florets.

2 Meanwhile, divide the cauliflower into about ½-inch/ 1-cm florets and blanch in a large saucepan of boiling salted water for 3 minutes. Drain and plunge into iced water to prevent additional cooking, then drain again.

3 Heat the oil in a medium saucepan over medium heat. When hot, but not smoking, add the mustard seeds, then the cumin seeds. Remove from the heat and add the garlic and chiles. Return to a low heat and cook, stirring, until the garlic has a light brown tinge.

4 Stir in the turmeric, followed by the cauliflower and the potatoes. Add the salt, increase the heat slightly, and cook, stirring, until the vegetables are well blended with the spices and heated through.

5 Stir in the cilantro, remove from the heat, and serve immediately.

garden peas & paneer in chili-tomato sauce

ingredients

serves 4

4 tbsp sunflower oil or olive oil
9 oz/250 g paneer, cut into
　1-inch/2.5-cm cubes
4 green cardamom pods, bruised
2 bay leaves
1 onion, finely chopped
2 tsp garlic paste
2 tsp ginger paste
2 tsp ground coriander
½ tsp ground turmeric
½–1 tsp chili powder
5½ oz/150 g canned chopped
　tomatoes
scant 2 cups warm water,
　plus 2 tbsp
1 tsp salt, or to taste
1¼ cups frozen peas
½ tsp garam masala
2 tbsp light cream
2 tbsp chopped fresh cilantro
　leaves

method

1 Heat 2 tablespoons of the oil in a medium nonstick saucepan over medium heat. Add the paneer and cook, stirring frequently, for 3–4 minutes, or until evenly browned. Remove and drain on paper towels.

2 Add the remaining oil to the saucepan and reduce the heat to low. Add the cardamom pods and bay leaves and let sizzle gently for 20–25 seconds. Add the onion, increase the heat to medium, and cook, stirring frequently, for 4–5 minutes, until the onion is softened. Add the garlic and ginger pastes and cook, stirring frequently, until the onion is a pale golden color.

3 Add the coriander, turmeric, and chili powder and cook, stirring, for 1 minute. Add the tomatoes and cook, stirring, for 4–5 minutes. Add the 2 tablespoons of warm water and cook, stirring, for 3 minutes, or until the oil separates from the spice paste.

4 Add the scant 2 cups of warm water and salt. Bring to a boil, then reduce the heat to low and simmer, uncovered, for 7–8 minutes. Add the paneer and peas and simmer for 5 minutes. Stir in the garam masala, cream, and fresh cilantro and remove from the heat. Serve immediately.

spinach & paneer

ingredients

serves 4

6 tbsp ghee or peanut oil
12 oz/350 g paneer, cut into
    ½-inch/1-cm pieces
1½ tbsp garlic and ginger paste
1 fresh green chile, seeded if you
    like, and chopped
4 tbsp water
1 onion, finely chopped
1 lb 5 oz/600 g fresh spinach
    leaves, any thick stems
    removed and rinsed
¼ tsp salt
¼ tsp garam masala
4 tbsp heavy cream
lemon wedges, to serve

method

1 Melt the ghee in a flameproof casserole or large skillet with a tight-fitting lid over medium–high heat. Add as many paneer pieces as will fit in a single layer without overcrowding the casserole and pan-fry for about 5 minutes, until golden brown on all sides. Use a slotted spoon to remove the paneer and drain it on crumpled paper towels. Continue, adding a little extra ghee, if necessary, until all the paneer is cooked.

2 Put the garlic and ginger paste and chile in a spice grinder or mortar and grind until a thick paste forms. Add the water and blend again.

3 Reheat the casserole with the ghee. Stir in the onion with the garlic and ginger paste mixture and sauté, stirring frequently, for 5–8 minutes, until the onion is soft, but not brown.

4 Add the spinach with just the water clinging to the leaves and the salt and stir around until it wilts. Reduce the heat to low, cover the casserole, and continue simmering until the spinach is soft.

5 Stir in the garam masala and cream, then gently return the paneer to the casserole. Simmer, stirring gently, until the paneer is heated through. Taste and adjust the seasoning, if necessary. Serve with lemon wedges for squeezing over.

bombay potatoes

ingredients

serves 6

1 lb 2 oz/500 g new potatoes, halved
1 tsp ground turmeric
4 tbsp ghee or vegetable oil
6 curry leaves
1 dried red chile
2 fresh green chiles, chopped
1/2 tsp nigella seeds
1 tsp mixed mustard and onion seeds
1/2 tsp cumin seeds
1/2 tsp fennel seeds
1/4 tsp asafetida
2 onions, chopped
5 tbsp chopped fresh cilantro
juice of 1/2 lime
salt

method

1 Place the potatoes in a large, heavy-bottom pan and pour in just enough cold water to cover. Add 1/2 teaspoon of the turmeric and a pinch of salt and bring to a boil. Let simmer for 10 minutes, or until tender, then drain and set aside until required.

2 Heat the ghee in a large, heavy-bottom skillet. Add the curry leaves and dried red chile and cook, stirring frequently, for a few minutes, or until the chile is blackened. Add the remaining turmeric, the fresh chiles, the nigella seeds, mustard, onion, cumin and fennel seeds, and the asafetida, onions, and fresh cilantro and cook, stirring constantly, for 5 minutes, or until the onions have softened.

3 Stir in the potatoes and cook over low heat, stirring frequently, for 10 minutes, or until heated through. Squeeze over the lime juice and serve.

potatoes with spiced spinach

ingredients

serves 4

12 oz/350 g young, waxy potatoes
9 oz/250 g spinach leaves,
    defrosted if frozen
3 tbsp sunflower oil or olive oil
1 large onion, finely sliced
1 fresh green chile, finely chopped
    (seeded if you like)
2 tsp garlic paste
2 tsp ginger paste
1 tsp ground coriander
½ tsp ground cumin
½ tsp chili powder
½ tsp ground turmeric
7 oz/200 g canned chopped
    tomatoes
½ tsp granulated sugar
1 tsp salt, or to taste
3 tbsp light cream

method

1 Cook the potatoes in their skins in a saucepan of boiling water for 20 minutes, or until tender. Drain, then soak in cold water for 30 minutes. Peel them, if you like, then halve or quarter.

2 Meanwhile, cook the spinach in a large saucepan of boiling water for 2 minutes, then drain. Transfer to a food processor and blend to a paste.

3 Heat 2 tablespoons of the oil in a medium saucepan over medium heat. Add the onion and cook, stirring, for 10–12 minutes, until browned, reducing the heat to low for the last 2–3 minutes. Remove from the heat and remove the excess oil from the onion. Drain on paper towels.

4 Return the pan to a low heat and add the remaining oil. Add the chile and garlic and ginger pastes and cook over low heat, stirring, for 2–3 minutes. Add the coriander, cumin, chili powder, and turmeric and cook, stirring, for 1 minute. Add the tomatoes, increase the heat to medium, and add the sugar. Cook, stirring, for 5–6 minutes.

5 Add the potatoes, spinach, salt, and reserved onion and cook, stirring, for 2–3 minutes. Stir in the cream and cook for 1 minute. Remove from the heat and serve immediately.

chickpeas in coconut milk

ingredients

serves 4

generous 1 cup water
10 oz/280 g potatoes, cut into
    ½-inch/1-cm cubes
14 oz/400 g canned chickpeas,
    drained and well rinsed
generous 1 cup canned
    coconut milk
1 tsp salt, or to taste
2 tbsp sunflower oil or olive oil
4 large garlic cloves, finely
    chopped or crushed
2 tsp ground coriander
½ tsp ground turmeric
½–1 tsp chili powder
juice of ½ lemon
Indian bread, to serve

method

1 Pour the water into a medium saucepan and add the potatoes. Bring to a boil, then reduce the heat to low and cook, covered, for 6–7 minutes, until the potatoes are al dente. Add the chickpeas and cook, uncovered, for 3–4 minutes, until the potatoes are tender. Add the coconut milk and salt and bring to a slow simmer.

2 Meanwhile, heat the oil in a small saucepan over low heat. Add the garlic and cook, stirring frequently, until it begins to brown. Add the coriander, turmeric, and chili powder and cook, stirring, for 25–30 seconds.

3 Fold the aromatic oil into the chickpea mixture. Stir in the lemon juice and remove from the heat. Serve immediately with Indian bread.

chickpeas with spiced tomatoes

ingredients

serves 4

6 tbsp vegetable oil
   or peanut oil
2 tsp cumin seeds
3 large onions, finely chopped
2 tsp garlic and ginger paste
2 small fresh green chiles, seeded
   and thinly sliced
1½ tsp amchoor
   (dried mango powder)
1½ tsp garam masala
¾ tsp ground asafetida
½ tsp ground turmeric
¼–1 tsp chili powder
3 large firm tomatoes, about
   1 lb/450 g, finely chopped
1 lb 12 oz/800 g canned
   chickpeas, rinsed and drained
6 tbsp water
10½ oz/300 g fresh spinach
   leaves, rinsed
½ tsp salt, or to taste

method

1 Heat the oil in a wok or large skillet over medium–high heat. Add the cumin seeds and stir around for 30 seconds, or until they brown and crackle, watching carefully because they can burn quickly.

2 Immediately stir in the onions, garlic and ginger paste, and chiles and sauté, stirring frequently, for 5–8 minutes, until the onions are golden.

3 Stir in the amchoor, garam masala, asafetida, turmeric, and chili powder. Add the tomatoes to the pan, stir them around the wok, and continue cooking, stirring frequently, until the sauce blends together and starts to brown slightly.

4 Stir in the chickpeas and water and bring to a boil. Reduce the heat to very low and use a wooden spoon or a potato masher to mash about one-quarter of the chickpeas, leaving the remainder whole.

5 Add the spinach to the pan with just the water clinging to the leaves and stir around until it wilts and is cooked. Stir in the salt, then taste and adjust the seasoning, adding more salt if necessary.

spiced black-eyed beans & mushrooms

ingredients

serves 4

1 onion, coarsely chopped

4 large garlic cloves, coarsely chopped

1-Inch/2.5-cm plece fresh glnger, coarsely chopped

4 tbsp sunflower oil or olive oil

1 tsp ground cumin

1 tsp ground coriander

½ tsp ground fennel

1 tsp ground turmeric

½–1 tsp chili powder

6 oz/175 g canned chopped tomatoes

14 oz/400 g canned black-eyed beans, drained and rinsed

4 oz/115 g large flat mushrooms, wiped and cut into bite-size pieces

½ tsp salt, or to taste

¾ cup warm water

1 tbsp chopped fresh mint

1 tbsp chopped fresh cilantro leaves

Indian bread, to serve

method

1 Process the onion, garlic, and ginger in a food processor or blender.

2 Heat the oil in a medium pan over medium–high heat and add the processed ingredients. Cook for 4–5 minutes, then add the cumin, coriander, fennel, turmeric, and chili powder. Stir-fry for about 1 minute, then add the tomatoes. Cook until the tomatoes are pulpy and the juice has evaporated.

3 Add the black-eyed beans, mushrooms, and salt. Stir well and pour in the warm water, then bring to a boil, cover the pan, and reduce the heat to low. Simmer for 8–10 minutes, stirring halfway through.

4 Stir in the chopped mint and cilantro and remove from the heat. Transfer to a serving dish and serve with Indian bread.

lentils with fresh chiles, mint & cilantro

ingredients

serves 4

⅓ cup split red lentils
(masoor dhal)
⅓ cup skinless split chickpeas
(chana dhal)
3 tbsp sunflower oil or olive oil
1 onion, finely chopped
2 tsp garlic paste
2 tsp ginger paste
2–3 fresh green chiles, chopped
(seeded if you like)
1 tsp ground cumin
2½ cups warm water
1 tsp salt, or to taste
1 tbsp chopped fresh mint
1 tbsp chopped fresh cilantro
leaves
4 tbsp unsalted butter
1 fresh green chile and 1 small
tomato, seeded and cut into
julienne strips, to garnish

method

1 Wash both types of lentil together until the water runs clear and let soak for 30 minutes.

2 Heat the oil in a medium saucepan, preferably nonstick, over medium heat and add the onion, garlic paste, ginger paste, and chiles. Stir-fry the mixture until it begins to brown.

3 Drain the lentils and add to the onion mixture together with the cumin. Reduce the heat to low and stir-fry for 2–3 minutes, then pour in the warm water. Bring to a boil, reduce the heat to low, cover, and simmer for 25–30 minutes.

4 Stir in the salt, mint, cilantro, and butter. Stir until the butter has melted, then remove from the heat. Serve garnished with the strips of chile and tomato.

sweet-&-sour lentils

ingredients

serves 4

1¼ cups split yellow lentils
   (chana dahl)
2 pints/1.2 litres/4 cups water
2 bay leaves, torn
3 fresh chiles, sliced once
½ tsp ground turmeric
½ tsp ground asafetida
3 tbsp vegetable or peanut oil
½ onion, finely chopped
¾-inch/2-cm piece fresh ginger,
   finely chopped
1 oz/30 g creamed coconut, grated
1 fresh green chile, seeded or not,
   to taste, and chopped
1½ tbsp sugar
1½ tbsp tamarind paste or
   tamarind chutney
½ tsp garam masala
¼ tsp ground cumin
¼ tsp ground coriander
salt

to garnish

1 tbsp ghee, melted, or vegetable
   or peanut oil
1 tsp garam masala
chopped fresh cilantro

method

1 Put the lentils and water in a large pan with a lid over high heat and bring to a boil, skimming the surface as necessary. When the foam stops rising, stir in the bay leaves, chiles, turmeric, and asafetida. Half cover the pan and let the lentils continue simmering for about 40 minutes, or until they are tender but not reduced to a mush, and all the liquid has been absorbed.

2 When the lentils are almost tender, heat the oil in a large, heavy-bottom pan over medium–high heat. Add the onion and ginger and sauté, stirring frequently, for 5–8 minutes.

3 Stir in the coconut, green chile, sugar, tamarind paste, garam masala, cumin, and coriander and stir for about 1 minute.

4 When the lentils are tender, add them, the bay leaves, chiles, and any liquid left in the pan to the spice mixture and stir around to blend together. Taste and add salt, if necessary, and extra sugar and tamarind, if desired.

5 Transfer the lentils to a serving dish and drizzle the hot ghee over the top. Sprinkle with garam masala and cilantro and serve immediately.

mixed lentils with five-spice seasoning

ingredients

serves 4

generous ½ cup split red lentils (masoor dhal)

generous ½ cup skinless split mung beans (mung dhal)

3¾ cups water

1 tsp ground turmeric

1 tsp salt, or to taste

1 tbsp lemon juice

2 tbsp sunflower oil or olive oil

¼ tsp black mustard seeds

¼ tsp cumin seeds

¼ tsp nigella seeds

¼ tsp fennel seeds

4–5 fenugreek seeds

2–3 dried red chiles

1 small tomato, seeded and cut into strips, and fresh cilantro sprigs, to garnish

Indian bread, to serve

method

1 Mix the lentils and beans together and wash until the water runs clear. Place the water in a saucepan over medium heat, bring to a boil, then add the lentils and beans. Bring to a boil, then reduce the heat slightly. Boil for 5–6 minutes, and when the foam subsides, add the turmeric, reduce the heat to low, cover, and cook for 20 minutes. Add the salt and lemon juice and beat the dhal with a wire whisk, adding a little more hot water if the dhal is too thick.

2 Heat the oil in a small saucepan over medium heat. When hot, but not smoking, add the mustard seeds. As soon as they begin to pop, reduce the heat to low and add the cumin seeds, nigella seeds, fennel seeds, fenugreek seeds, and dried chiles. Let the spices sizzle until the seeds begin to pop and the chiles have blackened. Pour the contents of the pan over the lentils, scraping off all the residue from the bottom of the pan.

3 Turn off the heat and keep the pan covered until you are ready to serve. Transfer to a serving dish and garnish with tomato strips and cilantro sprigs. Serve with Indian bread.

snacks & accompaniments

onion bhajis

ingredients

serves 4

generous 1 cup chickpea flour
1 tsp salt, or to taste
small pinch of baking soda
¼ cup ground rice
1 tsp fennel seeds
1 tsp cumin seeds
2 fresh green chiles, finely chopped
   (seeded if you like)
2 large onions, about 14 oz/400 g,
   sliced into half-rings and
   separated
1 cup fresh cilantro, including the
   tender stalks, finely chopped
scant 1 cup water
sunflower oil or olive oil,
   for deep-frying
tomato or mango chutney,
   to serve

method

1 Sift the chickpea flour into a large bowl and add the salt, baking soda, ground rice, and fennel and cumin seeds. Mix together thoroughly, then add the chiles, onions, and cilantro. Gradually pour in the water and mix until a thick batter is formed and all the other ingredients are thoroughly coated with it.

2 Heat enough oil for deep-frying in a wok, deep saucepan, or deep-fat fryer over medium heat to 350°F/180°C, or until a cube of bread browns in 30 seconds. If the oil is not hot enough, the bhajis will be soggy. Add as many small amounts (about 1/2 tablespoon) of the batter as will fit in a single layer, without overcrowding. Reduce the heat slightly and cook the bhajis for 8–10 minutes, until golden brown and crisp.

3 Remove and drain on paper towels. Keep hot in a low oven while you cook the remaining batter.

4 Serve hot with chutney.

golden cauliflower pakoras

ingredients

serves 4

vegetable or groundnut oil,
  for deep-frying
14 oz/400 g cauliflower florets
chutney, to serve

batter

5 oz/140 g chickpea flour
2 tsp ground coriander
1 tsp garam masala
1 tsp salt
½ tsp ground turmeric
pinch of chilli powder
½ oz/15 g ghee, melted,
  or 1 tbsp vegetable oil
1 tsp lemon juice
150 ml/5 fl oz cold water
2 tsp nigella seeds

method

1 To make the batter, stir the chickpea flour, coriander, garam masala, salt, turmeric, and chili powder into a large bowl. Make a well in the center, add the ghee and lemon juice with 2 tablespoons of the water, and stir together to make a thick batter.

2 Slowly beat in enough of the remaining water with an electric handheld mixer or a whisk to make a smooth batter about the same thickness as heavy cream. Stir in the nigella seeds. Cover the bowl and let stand for at least 30 minutes.

3 When you are ready to cook, heat enough oil for deep-frying in a kadhai, wok, deep-fat fryer, or large heavy-bottom pan until it reaches 350°F/180°C, or until a cube of bread browns in 30 seconds. Dip one cauliflower floret at a time into the batter and let any excess batter fall back into the bowl, then drop it into the hot oil. Add a few more dipped florets, without overcrowding the pan, and cook for about 3 minutes, or until golden brown and crisp.

4 Use a slotted spoon to remove the fritters from the oil and drain well on crumpled paper towels. Continue cooking until all the cauliflower florets and batter have been used. Serve the hot fritters with chutney for dipping.

vegetable samosas

ingredients

makes 12

3 tbsp sunflower oil or olive oil
½ tsp black mustard seeds
1 tsp cumin seeds
1 tsp fennel seeds
1 onion, finely chopped
2 fresh green chiles, finely chopped
(seeded if you like)
2 tsp ginger paste
½ tsp ground turmeric
1 tsp ground coriander
1 tsp ground cumin
½ tsp chili powder
12 oz/350 g boiled potatoes,
cut into bite-size pieces
scant 1 cup frozen peas, defrosted
1 tsp salt, or to taste
2 tbsp chopped fresh cilantro
leaves
12 sheets filo dough, about 11 x 7
inches/28 x 18 cm
4 tbsp butter, melted, plus extra
for greasing
chutney, for serving

method

1 Heat the oil in a saucepan over medium heat and add the mustard seeds, followed by the cumin and fennel seeds. Add the onion, chiles, and ginger paste and cook, stirring frequently, for 5–6 minutes.

2 Add the ground spices and cook, stirring, for 1 minute. Add the potatoes, peas, and salt and stir until the vegetables are thoroughly coated with the spices. Stir in the cilantro and remove from the heat. Let cool completely.

3 Line a baking sheet with parchment paper. Place a sheet of filo dough on a board and brush well with the melted butter. Keep the remaining filo dough sheets covered with a moist cloth or plastic wrap. Fold the buttered filo dough sheet in half lengthwise, brush with some more melted butter, and fold lengthwise again.

4 Place 1 tablespoon of the vegetable filling on the bottom right-hand corner of the filo dough sheet and fold over to form a triangle. Continue folding to the top of the sheet, maintaining the shape. Transfer to the prepared baking sheet and brush with melted butter. Repeat with the rest of the filo dough and filling.

5 Bake in a preheated oven, 350°F/180°C, for 20 minutes, or until browned. Serve hot with chutney.

deep-fried potato balls

ingredients

serves 4

1 lb/450 g potatoes, boiled
   and diced
1 onion, chopped
1-inch/2.5-cm piece fresh ginger,
   finely chopped
1 fresh green chile, seeded and
   finely chopped
1 tbsp chopped fresh cilantro
1 tbsp lemon juice
2 tsp aamchoor (dried mango
   powder)
vegetable oil, for deep-frying
salt
chutney, to serve

batter

¾ cup chickpea flour
¼ tsp baking powder
¼ tsp chili powder
about ⅔ cup water
salt

method

1 To make the batter, sift the flour, baking powder, chili powder, and a pinch of salt into a bowl. Gradually, stir in enough cold water to make a smooth batter. Cover with plastic wrap and set aside.

2 Place the potatoes, onion, ginger, chile, cilantro, lemon juice, and aamchoor into a separate bowl and season with salt to taste. Mix together well with a wooden spoon, breaking up the potatoes. Break off small pieces of the mixture and form into balls between the palms of your hands.

3 Heat the vegetable oil in a deep-fat fryer or heavy-bottom pan to 350–375°F/180–190°C, or until a cube of bread browns in 30 seconds. When the oil is hot, dip the potato balls in the batter, using a fork, and add to the oil, in batches. Deep-fry for 3–4 minutes, until golden brown. Remove with a slotted spoon and drain on paper towels. Keep each batch warm while you cook the remainder. Serve hot, with chutney.

spicy crêpes

ingredients

serves 6

5 oz/140 g/generous ¾ cup
  basmati rice, soaked for 2–3
  hours in cold water and
  drained
5 oz/140 g/generous ¾ cup black
  lentils, soaked for 2–3 hours in
  cold water and drained
2 fresh green chiles, seeded
  and finely chopped
1 tsp dark brown sugar
1¼ cups water
2 lb 12 oz/1.25 kg potatoes
3 tbsp grated fresh coconut
1-inch/2.5-cm piece fresh ginger,
  finely chopped
4 tbsp ghee or vegetable oil,
  plus extra for cooking
2 tsp black mustard seeds
2 tsp cumin seeds
1 tsp ground turmeric
3 tbsp chopped fresh cilantro
fresh mint sprigs, to garnish
salt
chutney, to serve

method

1 Place the rice and lentils in a food processor and process until ground. Pour into a bowl. Stir in half the chiles, the sugar, and a pinch of salt. Gradually add the water and mix to a smooth batter. Cover and let stand in a warm place overnight.

2 Cook the potatoes in lightly salted boiling water for 20–25 minutes, or until tender. Drain and mash. Mix the remaining chiles, coconut, and ginger to a paste.

3 Heat the ghee in a large, heavy-bottom skillet, add the mustard and cumin seeds, and stir until they give off their aroma. Stir in the coconut and ginger paste and cook for 1 minute, then add the mashed potatoes, turmeric, and cilantro and cook, stirring, for 5 minutes. Remove from the heat.

4 Heat a little ghee in an 8-inch/20-cm skillet. Stir the batter. Pour one sixth into the skillet, tilting the skillet to spread it over the bottom. Cook for 1–2 minutes, or until the underside is golden. Flip over and cook the other side for 2 minutes. Transfer to a plate and keep warm while you cook the remaining crêpes, adding more ghee as required. Divide the filling between the crêpes and fold in half. Return them to the skillet, in batches, and cook for 30 seconds on each side. Garnish with fresh mint sprigs and serve with chutney.

plantain chips

ingredients

serves 4

4 ripe plantains
1 tsp mild, medium, or hot
    curry powder, to taste
vegetable or peanut oil,
    for deep-frying
mango chutney, to serve

method

1 Peel the plantains, then cut crosswise into ⅛-inch/ 3-mm slices. Put the slices in a bowl, sprinkle over the curry powder, and use your hands to toss them lightly together.

2 Heat enough oil for deep-frying in a wok, deep-fat fryer, or large, heavy-bottom pan to 350°F/180°C, or until a cube of bread browns in 30 seconds. Add as many plantain slices as will fit in the pan without overcrowding and cook for 2 minutes, or until golden.

3 Remove the plantain chips from the pan with a slotted spoon and drain well on crumpled paper towels. Serve hot with mango chutney.

spiced basmati rice

ingredients

serves 4–6

scant 1¼ cups basmati rice
2 tbsp ghee or vegetable oil
5 green cardamom pods, bruised
5 cloves
½ cinnamon stick
1 tsp fennel seeds
½ tsp black mustard seeds
2 bay leaves
2 cups water
1½ tsp salt, or to taste
2 tbsp chopped fresh cilantro
salt and pepper

method

1 Rinse the basmati rice in several changes of water until the water runs clear, then let soak for 30 minutes. Drain and set aside until ready to cook.

2 Melt the ghee in a flameproof casserole or a large saucepan with a tight-fitting lid over medium–high heat. Add the spices and bay leaves and stir for 30 seconds. Stir the rice into the casserole so the grains are coated with ghee. Stir in the water and salt and bring to a boil.

3 Reduce the heat to as low as possible and cover the casserole tightly. Simmer, without lifting the lid, for 8–10 minutes, until the grains are tender and all the liquid is absorbed.

4 Turn off the heat and use two forks to mix in the cilantro. Adjust the seasoning, adding salt and pepper if necessary. Re-cover the pan and let stand for 5 minutes.

mint & cilantro rice with toasted pine nuts

ingredients

serves 4

generous 1 cup basmati rice

2 tbsp sunflower oil or olive oil

2-inch/5-cm piece cinnamon
  stick, broken in half

4 green cardamom pods, bruised

2 star anise

2 bay leaves

2 cups lukewarm water

good pinch of saffron threads,
  pounded and soaked in
  2 tbsp hot milk

3 tbsp fresh cilantro leaves,
  finely chopped

2 tbsp fresh mint leaves, finely
  chopped, or 1 tsp dried mint

1 tsp salt, or to taste

scant 1/4 cup pine nuts

method

1 Wash the rice in several changes of cold water until the water runs clear. Let soak in fresh cold water for 20 minutes, then let drain in a colander.

2 Heat the oil in a medium heavy-bottom saucepan over low heat. Add the cinnamon, cardamom, star anise, and bay leaves and let sizzle gently for 20–25 seconds. Add the rice and stir well to ensure that the grains are coated with the flavored oil.

3 Add the water, stir once, and bring to a boil. Add the saffron and milk, cilantro, mint, and salt and boil for 2–3 minutes. Cover tightly, reduce the heat to very low, and cook for 7–8 minutes. Turn off the heat and let stand, covered, for 7–8 minutes.

4 Meanwhile, preheat a small heavy-bottom skillet over medium heat, add the pine nuts, and cook, stirring, until lightly toasted. Alternatively, cook in a foil-covered broiler pan under a preheated medium broiler, turning 2–3 times, until lightly toasted. Transfer to a plate and let cool.

5 Add half the toasted pine nuts to the rice and fluff up the rice with a fork. Transfer to a serving dish, garnish with the remaining pine nuts, and serve immediately.

lemon-laced basmati rice

ingredients

serves 4

generous 1 cup basmati rice
2 tbsp sunflower oil or olive oil
½ tsp black or brown mustard
    seeds
10–12 curry leaves, preferably
    fresh
scant ¼ cup cashews
¼ tsp ground turmeric
1 tsp salt, or to taste
2 cups hot water
2 tbsp lemon juice
1 tbsp snipped fresh chives,
    to garnish

method

1 Wash the rice in several changes of cold water until
   the water runs clear. Let soak in fresh cold water for
   20 minutes, then let drain in a colander.

2 Heat the oil in a nonstick saucepan over medium
   heat. When hot, but not smoking, add the mustard
   seeds, followed by the curry leaves and the cashews
   (in that order).

3 Stir in the turmeric, quickly followed by the rice and
   salt. Cook, stirring, for 1 minute, then add the hot water
   and lemon juice. Stir once, bring to a boil, and boil for
   2 minutes. Cover tightly, reduce the heat to very low,
   and cook for 8 minutes. Turn off the heat and let stand,
   covered, for 6–7 minutes.

4 Fork through the rice and transfer to a serving dish.
   Garnish with the chives and serve immediately.

coconut rice

ingredients

serves 4–6

8 oz/225 g/scant 1¼ cups
    basmati rice
2 tbsp mustard oil
2¼ oz/60 g/cups coconut
    cream
1½ tsp salt

method

1 Rinse the rice in several changes of water until the water runs clear, then let soak for 30 minutes. Drain and set aside until ready to cook.

2 Heat the oil in a large skillet or saucepan with a tight-fitting lid over high heat until it smokes. Turn off the heat and let the oil cool completely.

3 When you are ready to cook, reheat the oil over medium–high heat. Add the rice and stir until all the grains are coated in oil. Add the coconut cream and bring to a boil.

4 Reduce the heat to as low as possible, stir in the salt, and cover the skillet tightly. Simmer, without lifting the lid, for 8–10 minutes, until the grains are tender and all the liquid has been absorbed.

5 Turn off the heat and use two forks to mix the rice. Re-cover the pan and let the rice stand for 5 minutes.

spiced basmati pilaf

ingredients

serves 4–6

2½ cups basmati rice
6 oz/175 g head of broccoli
6 tbsp vegetable oil
2 large onions, chopped
8 oz/225 g button mushrooms,
    sliced
2 garlic cloves, crushed
6 green cardamom pods, bruised
6 whole cloves
8 black peppercorns
1 cinnamon stick or piece
    of cassia bark
1 tsp ground turmeric
5 cups boiling vegetable stock
    or water
⅓ cup seedless raisins
½ cup unsalted pistachios,
    coarsely chopped
salt and pepper

method

1 Place the rice in a strainer and wash well under cold running water. Drain. Trim off most of the broccoli stalk and cut into small florets, then quarter the stalk lengthwise and cut diagonally into 1-cm/½-inch pieces.

2 Heat the oil in a large pan. Add the onions and broccoli stalks and cook over low heat, stirring frequently, for 3 minutes. Add the mushrooms, rice, garlic, and spices and cook for 1 minute, stirring, until the rice is coated in oil.

3 Add the boiling stock and season to taste with salt and pepper. Stir in the broccoli florets and return the mixture to a boil. Cover, reduce the heat, and cook over low heat for 15 minutes without uncovering the pan.

4 Remove the pan from the heat and let the pilaf stand for 5 minutes without uncovering. Remove the whole spices, add the raisins and pistachios, and gently fork through to fluff up the grains. Serve the pilaf hot.

chapatis

ingredients

makes 16

scant 3 cups chapati flour (atta),
    plus extra for dusting
1 tsp salt
½ tsp granulated sugar
2 tbsp sunflower oil or olive oil
generous 1 cup lukewarm water

method

1 Mix the chapati flour, salt, and sugar together in a large bowl. Add the oil and work well into the flour mixture with your fingertips. Gradually add the water, mixing at the same time. When the dough is formed, transfer to a counter and knead for 4–5 minutes. The dough is ready when all the excess moisture is absorbed by the flour. Alternatively, mix the dough in a food processor. Wrap the dough in plastic wrap and let rest for 30 minutes.

2 Divide the dough in half, then cut each half into 8 equal-size pieces. Form each piece into a ball and flatten into a round cake. Dust each cake lightly in the flour and roll out to a 6-inch/15-cm circle. Keep the remaining cakes covered while you are working on one. The chapatis will cook better when freshly rolled out, so roll out and cook one at a time.

3 Preheat a heavy-bottom cast-iron griddle (tawa) or a large heavy-bottom skillet over medium–high heat. Put a chapati on the griddle and cook for 30 seconds. Using a thin spatula, turn over and cook until bubbles begin to appear on the surface. Turn over again. Press the edges down gently with a clean cloth to encourage the chapati to puff up. Cook until brown patches appear on the underside. Remove from the pan and keep hot by wrapping in a piece of foil lined with paper towels. Repeat with the remaining dough cakes.

chile-cilantro naan

ingredients

makes 8

3¼ cups all-purpose flour
2 tsp sugar
1 tsp salt
1 tsp baking powder
1 egg
generous 1 cup milk
2 tbsp sunflower oil or olive oil,
    plus extra for oiling
2 fresh red chiles, chopped
    (seeded if you like)
1 cup fresh cilantro leaves,
    chopped
2 tbsp butter, melted

method

1 Sift the flour, sugar, salt, and baking powder together into a large bowl. Whisk the egg and milk together, then add to the flour and mix until a dough is formed.

2 Transfer the dough to a counter, make a depression in the center of the dough, and add the oil. Knead for 3–4 minutes, until you have a smooth and pliable dough. Wrap the dough in plastic wrap and let rest for 1 hour. Divide the dough into 8 equal-size pieces; form each piece into a ball, and flatten into a thick cake. Cover with plastic wrap and let rest for 10–15 minutes.

3 Preheat the broiler to high. Line a broiler pan with foil and brush with oil. Roll each flattened cake into a 5-inch/13-cm circle and pull the lower end gently. Carefully roll out again, maintaining the teardrop shape, to about 9 inches/23 cm in diameter.

4 Mix the chiles and cilantro together, then spread on the surface of the naans. Press gently so the mixture sticks to the dough. Transfer a naan to the prepared broiler pan and cook for 1 minute, or until slightly puffed and brown patches appear on the surface. Turn over and cook the other side for 45–50 seconds, until lightly browned. Remove from the broiler and brush with the melted butter. Wrap in a dish towel while you cook the remaining naans.

pooris

ingredients

makes 12

1½ cups whole-wheat flour, sifted,
   plus extra for dusting
½ teaspoon salt
2 tbsp ghee, melted
⅓–⅔ cup water
vegetable oil or peanut oil,
   for deep-frying

method

1 Put the flour and salt into a bowl and drizzle the ghee over the surface. Gradually stir in the water until a stiff dough forms. Turn out the dough onto a lightly floured counter and knead for 10 minutes, or until it is smooth and elastic. Shape the dough into a ball and place it in a clean bowl, then cover with a damp dish towel and let rest for 20 minutes.

2 Divide the dough into 12 equal-size pieces and roll each into a ball. Working with one ball of dough at a time, flatten the dough between your palms, then thinly roll it out on a lightly floured counter into a 5-inch/13-cm circle. Continue until all the dough balls are rolled out.

3 Heat at least 3 inches/7.5 cm oil in a wok, deep-fat fryer, or large skillet until it reaches 350°F/180°C, or until a cube of bread browns in 30 seconds. Drop a poori into the hot oil and deep-fry for about 10 seconds, or until it puffs up. Use 2 large spoons to flip the poori over and spoon some hot oil over the top.

4 Use the 2 spoons to lift the poori from the oil. Drain the poori on crumpled paper towels and serve immediately. Continue until all the pooris are cooked, making sure the oil returns to the correct temperature before you add another poori.

cucumber raita

ingredients

serves 4–5

1 small cucumber
¾ cup plain yogurt
¼ tsp sugar
¼ tsp salt
1 tsp cumin seeds
10–12 black peppercorns
¼ tsp paprika

method

1 Peel the cucumber and scoop out the seeds. Cut the flesh into bite-size pieces and set aside.

2 Put the yogurt in a bowl and beat with a fork until smooth. Add the sugar and salt and mix well.

3 Preheat a small heavy-bottom saucepan over medium–high heat. When the pan is hot, turn off the heat and add the cumin seeds and peppercorns. Stir for 40–50 seconds, until they release their aroma. Remove from the pan and let cool for 5 minutes, then crush in a mortar with a pestle or on a hard surface with a rolling pin.

4 Set aside ¼ teaspoon of this mixture and stir the remainder into the yogurt. Add the cucumber and stir to mix. Transfer the raita to a serving dish and sprinkle with the reserved toasted spices and the paprika.

mint & spinach chutney

Not very good

ingredients

serves 4–6

2 oz/55 g tender fresh spinach
  leaves
3 tbsp fresh mint leaves
2 tbsp chopped fresh cilantro
  leaves
1 small red onion, coarsely
  chopped
1 small garlic clove, chopped
1 fresh green chile, chopped
  (seeded if you like)
2½ tsp granulated sugar
1 tbsp tamarind juice or juice
  of ½ lemon

method

1 Put all the ingredients in a blender or food processor and blend until smooth, adding a little water to enable the blades to move, if necessary.

2 Transfer to a serving bowl, cover, and chill in the refrigerator for at least 30 minutes.

tomato kachumbar

ingredients

serves 6

4 oz/125 ml/½ cup lime juice
½ tsp sugar
6 tomatoes, chopped
½ cucumber, chopped
8 scallions, chopped
1 fresh green chile, seeded
    and chopped
1 tbsp chopped fresh cilantro
1 tbsp chopped fresh mint
salt

method

1 Mix the lime juice, sugar, and a pinch of salt together in a large bowl and stir until the sugar has completely dissolved.

2 Add the tomatoes, cucumber, scallions, chile, cilantro, and mint and toss well to mix.

3 Cover with plastic wrap and let chill in the refrigerator for at least 30 minutes. Toss the vegetables before serving.

cilantro chutney

ingredients

serves 4–6

1½ tbsp lemon juice
1½ tbsp water
3 oz/85 g fresh cilantro leaves
  and stems, coarsely chopped
2 tbsp chopped fresh coconut
1 small shallot, very finely chopped
¼-inch/5-mm piece fresh ginger,
  chopped
1 fresh green chile, seeded
  and chopped
½ tsp sugar
½ tsp salt
pinch of pepper

method

1 Put the lemon juice and water in a small food processor, add half the cilantro, and process until it is blended and a slushy paste forms. Gradually add the remaining cilantro and process until it is all blended, scraping down the sides of the processor, if necessary. If you don't have a processor that will cope with this small amount, use a pestle and mortar, adding the cilantro in small amounts.

2 Add the remaining ingredients and continue blending until they are all finely chopped and blended. Taste and adjust any of the seasonings, if you like. Transfer to a nonmetallic bowl, cover, and chill for up to 3 days before serving.

mango chutney

ingredients

serves 4–6

1 large mango, about 14 oz/
    400 g, peeled, pitted,
    and finely chopped
2 tbsp lime juice
1 tbsp vegetable oil or peanut oil
2 shallots, finely chopped
1 garlic clove, finely chopped
2 fresh green chiles, seeded
    and finely sliced
1 tsp black mustard seeds
1 tsp coriander seeds
5 tbsp grated jaggery or light
    brown sugar
5 tbsp white wine vinegar
1 tsp salt
pinch of ground ginger

method

1 Put the mango in a nonmetallic bowl with the lime juice and set aside.

2 Heat the oil in a large skillet or pan over medium–high heat. Add the shallots and sauté for 3 minutes. Add the garlic and chiles and stir for an additional 2 minutes, or until the shallots are softened but not browned. Add the mustard seeds and coriander seeds, then stir.

3 Add the mango to the pan with the jaggery, vinegar, salt, and ginger and stir. Reduce the heat to its lowest setting and simmer for 10 minutes, until the liquid thickens and the mango becomes sticky.

4 Remove from the heat and let cool completely. Transfer to an airtight container, cover, and chill for 3 days before using.

lime pickle

ingredients

serves 6–8

12 limes, halved and seeded
4 oz/115 g salt
2½ oz/70 g chili powder
1 oz/25 g mustard powder
1 oz/25 g ground fenugreek
1 tbsp ground turmeric
1¼ cups mustard oil
½ oz/15 g yellow mustard
  seeds, crushed
½ tsp asafetida

method

1 Cut each lime half into 4 pieces and pack them into a large sterilized jar, sprinkling over the salt at the same time. Cover the limes and let stand in a warm place for 10–14 days, or until they have turned brown and are softened.

2 Mix the chili powder, mustard powder, fenugreek, and turmeric together in a small bowl and add to the jar of limes. Stir to mix, then re-cover and let stand for 2 days.

3 Transfer the lime mixture to a heatproof bowl. Heat the oil in a heavy-bottom skillet. Add the mustard seeds and asafetida to the skillet and cook, stirring continuously, until the oil is very hot and just starting to smoke.

4 Pour the oil and spices over the limes and mix well. Cover and let cool. When cool, pack the limes into a sterilized jar. Seal and store in a sunny place for a week before serving.

desserts

indian rice dessert

ingredients

serves 4

3 tbsp ghee or unsalted butter
generous ½ cup ground rice
¼ cup slivered almonds
scant ¼ cup seedless raisins
2½ cups whole milk
2 cups evaporated milk
¼ cup superfine sugar
12 plumped dried apricots, sliced
good pinch of saffron threads,
    pounded and soaked in
    2 tbsp hot milk
1 tsp freshly ground cardamom
    seeds
½ tsp freshly grated nutmeg
2 tbsp rose water

to decorate

¼ cup walnut pieces
2 tbsp shelled unsalted pistachios

method

1 Set aside 2 teaspoons of the ghee and melt the remainder in a heavy-bottom saucepan over low heat. Add the ground rice, almonds, and raisins and cook, stirring, for 2 minutes. Add the whole milk, increase the heat to medium, and cook, stirring, until it begins to bubble gently. Reduce the heat to low and cook, stirring frequently, for 10–12 minutes, to prevent the mixture from sticking to the bottom of the pan.

2 Add the evaporated milk, sugar, and apricots, setting a few slices aside to decorate. Cook, stirring, until the mixture thickens to the consistency of a pouring custard.

3 Add the saffron and milk mixture, cardamom, nutmeg, and rose water, stir to distribute well, and remove from the heat. Let cool, then cover and chill in the refrigerator for at least 2 hours.

4 Melt the reserved ghee in a small saucepan over low heat. Add the walnuts and cook, stirring, until they brown a little. Remove and drain on paper towels. Brown the pistachios in the saucepan, remove, and drain on paper towels. Let the pistachios cool, then lightly crush.

5 Serve the dessert decorated with the fried nuts and the reserved apricot slices.

sago & coconut dessert

ingredients

serves 4

½ fresh coconut
1 cup water
3½ cups milk
scant ½ cup superfine sugar
2 tbsp raisins
scant ⅓ cup sago
seeds from 6–8 green
    cardamom pods
¼ cup slivered almonds,
    to decorate

method

1 To prepare the coconut milk, remove the flesh from the coconut shell and grate it. Place in a food processor or blender, add the water, and process until smooth. Strain into a pitcher, pressing down on the coconut with the back of a wooden spoon. Discard the contents of the strainer and reserve the coconut milk.

2 Bring the 3½ cups milk to a boil in a large heavy-bottom pan and continue to boil until it has reduced to 2½ cups. Reduce the heat, add the sugar, and stir until dissolved. Stir in the raisins and sago. Let simmer gently for 6–8 minutes, or until the sago is cooked.

3 Remove the pan from the heat and stir in the coconut milk and cardamom seeds, then pour into individual serving dishes. Sprinkle with the almonds and let cool before serving.

mango kulfi

ingredients

serves 6–8

generous 1½ cups canned
    evaporated milk
1¼ cups light cream
¼ cup ground almonds
½–⅓ cup granulated sugar
1 lb/450 g mango puree
1 tsp freshly ground cardamom
    seeds
scant ¼ cup shelled unsalted
    pistachios, to decorate

method

1 Pour the evaporated milk and cream into a heavy-bottom saucepan and stir to mix. Put over medium heat. Mix the ground almonds and sugar together, then add to the milk mixture. Cook, stirring, for 6–8 minutes, until the mixture thickens slightly.

2 Remove from the heat and let the mixture cool completely, stirring from time to time to prevent a skin from forming. When completely cold, stir in the mango puree and ground cardamom.

3 Meanwhile, preheat a small saucepan over medium heat, add the pistachios, and toast for 2–3 minutes. Let cool, then lightly crush. Store in an airtight container until required.

4 Kulfi is set in traditional conical-shape plastic or steel molds, which you can buy from Asian stores, but you can use decorative individual molds or popsicle molds instead. Fill the containers of your choice with the kulfi mixture and freeze for 5–6 hours. Transfer the kulfi to the refrigerator for 40 minutes, then invert onto serving dishes. Serve sprinkled with the crushed pistachios to decorate.

saffron & almond kulfi

ingredients

makes 4

5 tbsp milk
1 tbsp ground rice
½ tbsp ground almonds
8 fl oz/225 ml/1 cup canned
    evaporated milk
½ tsp saffron threads, toasted
    in a dry skillet over a high heat
8 fl oz/225 ml/1 cup heavy cream
2 tbsp superfine sugar
2 tbsp chopped toasted blanched
    almonds, to serve

method

1 Put the milk in the skillet over medium–high heat, add the saffron threads, and heat just until small bubbles appear around the edge. Remove the pan from the heat and let the saffron steep for at least 15 minutes. Meanwhile, combine the ground rice and ground almonds in a heatproof bowl. Put a flat freezerproof container into the freezer.

2 Reheat the milk and saffron just until small bubbles appear, then slowly beat the milk into the almond mixture, until smooth. Pour the evaporated milk into a pan and bring to a boil, stirring. Remove the pan and stir into the milk mixture. Stir in the cream and sugar.

3 Return the pan to medium heat and simmer, stirring constantly, for 5–10 minutes, until it thickens, but do not boil. Remove the pan from the heat and set aside, stirring frequently, to cool. Pour the saffron mixture into the freezerproof bowl and freeze for 30 minutes, then beat to break up any ice crystals. Beat every 30 minutes, until the ice cream is thick and almost firm.

4 Divide the mixture among 4 kulfi molds or ramekins. Cover and freeze until solid. To serve, dip a dish towel in hot water, wring it out, and rub it around the sides of the molds or ramekins, then invert onto plates. Sprinkle with toasted almonds and serve.

almond & pistachio dessert

ingredients

serves 2

5½ tbsp unsalted butter
2 cups ground almonds
7 oz/200 g/1 cup sugar
5 fl oz/150 ml/²/₃ cup light cream
8 almonds, chopped
10 pistachios, chopped

method

1 Melt the butter in a heavy-bottom pan, preferably nonstick, stirring well. Add the ground almonds, sugar, and cream, stirring well. Reduce the heat and stir constantly for 10–12 minutes, scraping the bottom of the pan.

2 Increase the heat until the mixture turns a little darker in color.

3 Transfer the almond mixture to a large, shallow serving dish and smooth the top with the back of a spoon.

4 Decorate the top of the dessert with the chopped almonds and pistachios. Let set for 1 hour, then cut into diamond shapes and serve cold.

carrot halva

ingredients

serves 4–6

4 tbsp ghee or unsalted butter
1-inch/2.5-cm piece cinnamon
    stick, halved
¼ cup slivered almonds
scant ¼ cup cashews
scant ¼ cup seedless raisins
8 carrots, grated
2½ cups whole milk
scant ¾ cup superfine sugar
½ tsp freshly ground cardamom
    seeds
½ tsp freshly grated nutmeg
2 fl oz/60 ml/¼ cup heavy cream
2 tbsp rose water
vanilla ice cream or whipped heavy
    cream, to serve

method

1 Melt the ghee in a heavy-bottom saucepan over low heat. Add the cinnamon stick and let sizzle gently for 25–30 seconds. Add the almonds and cashews and cook, stirring, until lightly browned. Remove about a dessertspoon of the nuts and set aside.

2 Add the raisins, carrots, milk, and sugar to the saucepan, increase the heat to medium, and bring the milk to boiling point. Continue to cook over low–medium heat for 15–20 minutes, until the milk evaporates completely, stirring frequently, and scraping and blending in any thickened milk that sticks to the side of the saucepan. Don't allow any milk that is stuck to the side to brown or burn, because this will give the dessert an unpleasant flavor.

3 Stir in the cardamom, nutmeg, cream, and rose water. Remove from the heat and let cool slightly, then serve topped with a scoop of vanilla ice cream or whipped heavy cream. Sprinkle over the reserved nuts to decorate.

shrikhand with pomegranate

ingredients

serves 4

4 cups plain yogurt
$\frac{1}{4}$ tsp saffron threads
2 tbsp milk
generous $\frac{1}{4}$ cup superfine sugar,
    or to taste
seeds from 2 green cardamom
    pods
2 pomegranates or other
    exotic fruit

method

1 Line a strainer set over a bowl with a piece of cheesecloth large enough to hang over the edge. Add the yogurt, then tie the corners of the cheesecloth into a tight knot and tie them to a faucet. Let the bundle hang over the sink for 4 hours, or until all the excess moisture drips away.

2 Put the saffron threads in a dry pan over high heat and toast, stirring frequently, until you can smell the aroma. Immediately turn them out of the pan. Put the milk in the pan, return the saffron threads, and warm just until bubbles appear around the edge, then set aside and let steep.

3 When the yogurt is thick and creamy, put it in a bowl, stir in the sugar, cardamom seeds, and saffron-and-milk mixture, and beat until smooth. Taste and add extra sugar, if desired. Cover and chill for at least 1 hour, until well chilled.

4 Meanwhile, to prepare the pomegranate seeds, cut the fruit in half and use a small teaspoon or your fingers to scoop out the seeds.

5 To serve, spoon the yogurt into individual bowls or plates and add the pomegranate seeds.

ginger ice cream with date & tamarind sauce

ingredients

serves 4–5

4 cups vanilla ice cream
2 tsp ground ginger
7 oz/200 g candied ginger,
   chopped, to serve

tamarind sauce

⅓ cup seedless raisins
½ cup pitted dried dates
generous 1 cup boiling water
2 rounded tsp tamarind
   concentrate or 3 tbsp
   tamarind juice
scant ¼ cup molasses sugar

method

1 Let the ice cream stand at room temperature for 35–40 minutes to soften, then transfer to a bowl. Add the ground ginger and beat well. Return the mixture to the carton and freeze for 3–4 hours.

2 Meanwhile, to make the sauce, put the raisins and dates in a heatproof bowl, pour over the boiling water, and let soak for 15–20 minutes. Transfer to a food processor, add the tamarind and sugar, and blend to a smooth paste. Transfer to a nonmetallic bowl and let cool.

3 Put scoops of the ice cream into serving dishes and drizzle over the sauce. Arrange 1 dessertspoon of candied ginger on top of each dessert and serve immediately. Serve any extra sauce separately.

sweet saffron rice with caramelized pineapple

ingredients

serves 4–6

4 tbsp ghee or unsalted butter

½ fresh pineapple (8 oz/225 g prepared weight) peeled, with eyes removed, and cut into bite-sized pieces

6 oz/175 g/¾–scant 1 cup superfine sugar

4 green cardamom pods, bruised

4 cloves

2 cinnamon sticks, each ½ inch/ 1 cm long

6 oz/175 g/scant 1 cup basmati rice

good pinch of saffron threads, pounded and soaked in 2 tbsp hot milk

10 fl oz/300 ml/1¼ cups warm water

2 oz/55 g/⅓ cup seedless raisins

1 oz/25 g/scant ¼ cup toasted slivered almonds, for decorating

light cream, for serving

method

1 Melt 1 tablespoon of the ghee in a large, heavy-bottom skillet over low heat. Add the pineapple, sprinkle with 2 tablespoons of the sugar, and increase the heat to high. Caramelize the pineapple, then remove from the heat.

2 Melt the remaining ghee. Add the cardamom pods, cloves, and cinnamon sticks and cook, stirring. Add the rice, increase the heat slightly, and cook, stirring, for 2–3 minutes. Add the saffron, milk and the warm water, boil for 2 minutes, then reduce the heat to low for 2–3 minutes. Remove from the heat.

3 Add one third of the rice to a lidded ovenproof dish. Top with one third of the raisins, followed by one third of the pineapple pieces and one third of the remaining sugar. Repeat twice more, finishing with a layer of raisins, pineapple, and sugar.

4 Soak a piece of wax paper, crumple it, then place loosely over the top layer. Cover with foil and seal the edges. Put the lid on and bake in the center of a preheated oven, 325°F/160°C, for 35–40 minutes. Turn off the oven and let the rice stand inside for 10–15 minutes. Decorate with the slivered almonds and serve with cream.

mango lassi

ingredients

serves 4–6

1 large mango, about
    10½ oz/300 g, peeled, pitted,
    and coarsely chopped
3 cups plain yogurt
generous 1 cup cold water
about 2 tbsp superfine sugar,
    or to taste
fresh lime juice, to taste
ice cubes
ground ginger, to decorate
    (optional)

method

1 Put the mango in a food processor or blender with the yogurt and process until smooth. Add the water and process again to blend.

2 The amount of sugar you will add depends on how sweet the mango is. Taste and stir in sugar to taste, then stir in the lime juice.

3 Fill 4–6 glasses with ice cubes and pour over the mango mixture. Lightly dust the top of each glass with ground ginger, if you like.

index

beef
- balti beef 58
- beef korma with almonds 62
- beef madras 60

carrot halva 198
cauliflower
- cauliflower & sweet potato curry 110
- cauliflower, eggplant & green bean korma 108
- garlic & chile-flavored potatoes with cauliflower 122
- golden cauliflower pakoras 148
chapatis 168
chicken
- balti chicken 14
- butter chicken 18
- chicken biryani 26
- chicken dopiaza 8
- chicken korma 10
- chicken tikka masala 16
- chicken with stir-fried spices 22
- cumin-scented chicken 24
- Kashmiri chicken 12
- silky chicken kabobs 30
- tandoori chicken 28
- wok-cooked chicken in tomato & fenugreek sauce 20
chickpeas with spiced tomatoes 134
cilantro chutney 180
coconut
- chickpeas in coconut milk 132
- coconut rice 164
- mussels in coconut sauce 92
- sago & coconut dessert 190
- shrimp in coconut milk with chiles & curry leaves 98
cucumber raita 174

eggplant
- cauliflower, eggplant & green bean korma 108

cumin-scented
- eggplant & potato curry 112

fish & seafood
- balti fish curry 80
- Bengali-style fish 74
- butterfish in chili yogurt 78
- fish in tomato & chili sauce with fried onion 84
- fish korma 86
- fish tikka 88
- Goan-style seafood curry 82
- steamed fish with cilantro chutney 76

ginger ice cream with date & tamarind sauce 202
green bean & potato curry 116

lamb
- Kashmiri lamb chops 52
- lamb dhansak 34
- lamb dopiaza 38
- lamb kabobs 50
- lamb pasanda 40
- lamb rogan josh 36
- lamb, tomato & eggplant curry 42
- lean lamb cooked in spinach 46
- marinated lamb brochettes 56
- meatballs in creamy cashew nut sauce 48
- Peshawar-style lamb curry 44
- sesame lamb chops 54
lentils
- lentils with fresh chiles, mint & cilantro 138
- mixed lentils with five-spice seasoning 142
- sweet-&-sour lentils 140
lime pickle 184

mango
- mango chutney 182
- mango kulfi 192
- mango lassi 206

mint & spinach chutney 176
mushroom bhaji 104
mussels
- mussels in coconut sauce 92
- mussels with mustard seeds & shallots 90

naan, chili-cilantro 170
nuts
- almond & pistachio dessert 196
- beef korma with almonds 62
- meatballs in creamy cashew nut sauce 48
- saffron & almond kulfi 194

okra stir-fried with onions 120
onion bhajis 146

paneer
- garden peas & paneer in chili-tomato sauce 124
- spinach & paneer 126
plantain chips 156
pooris 172
pork
- pork vindaloo 64
- pork with cinnamon & fenugreek 66
- railway pork & vegetables 70
- red curry pork with peppers 68
potatoes
- Bombay potatoes 128
- cauliflower & sweet potato curry 110
- cumin-scented eggplant & potato curry 112
- deep-fried potato balls 152
- garlic & chile-flavored potatoes with cauliflower 122
- green bean & potato curry 116
- potatoes with spiced spinach 130

rice
- coconut rice 164
- Indian rice dessert 188
- lemon-laced basmati rice 162
- mint & cilantro rice with toasted pine nuts 160
- spiced basmati rice 158
- spiced basmati pilaf 166
- sweet saffron rice with caramelized pineapple 204

sago & coconut dessert 190
samosas, vegetable 150
shrikhand with pomegranate 200
shrimp
- shrimp & pineapple tikka 94
- shrimp in coconut milk with chiles & curry leaves 98
- shrimp pooris 96
- tandoori shrimp 100
spiced black-eyed beans & mushrooms 136
spicy crêpes 154

tamarind
- ginger ice cream with date & tamarind sauce 202
tofu & vegetable curry 114
tomatoes
- chickpeas with spiced tomatoes 134
- fish in tomato & chili sauce with fried onion 84
- tomato kachumbar 178
- wok-cooked chicken in tomato & fenugreek sauce 20

vegetables
- vegetable korma 106
- vegetable sambar 118
- vegetable samosas 150